JOSEPH'S REDEMPTION

JOSEPH'S
REDEMPTION

Richard Malmed

Kravitz & Sons
INNOVATORS IN PUBLISHING, MARKETING AND ADVERTISING

Kravitz and Sons LLC
1301 Farmville Blvd, Suite 104
Greenville, NC 27834

Published by Kravitz and Sons LLC.

ISBN: 979-8-89639-060-2 (sc)
ISBN: 979-8-89639-059-6 (e)

Library of Congress Control Number: 2024926842

Because of the dynamic nature of the Internet, any web addresses or links contained in this book may have changed since publication and may no longer be valid. The views expressed in this work are solely those of the author and do not necessarily reflect the views of the publisher, and the publisher hereby disclaims any responsibility for them.

CONTENTS

In Prison

It was finally beginning to sink in I was in prison. I was in prison for a crime I did not commit. Slowly the months of denial began to fade. What was my first clue? As I lay on my back in the upper bed, I could not ignore the smell of the heavy disinfectant mixed with an overwhelming odor of urine. It was enough to make my eyes water. It may have been the loud rap music coming from the earphones of my cell mate in the lower bed as I tried to sleep. This was my first night in prison. The judge had ordered me locked up directly after sentencing. The prosecutor had reminded the judge there was an unaccounted for $3 million and I might flee to get it. The judge could not take the heat if I disappeared even though I had ample grounds for appeal. He wanted me to serve my time and he wanted to have it start now. It was probably because my law firm was behind it. They had accused me of stealing the $3 million from their escrow account from a large municipal bond financing. They had clout, I no longer did. I was a junior associate, they were a large prestigious firm. If they wanted justice they got it. But I hadn't done it. My lawyer had fought hard but never could get to the facts I needed. Someone had set me up.

As sleep would not come, I began to drift over my life and examine what had gone wrong. Tomorrow, I would be sent out to the prison where I would serve my sentence three to six years for embezzlement. At least three years in Graterford State Correctional Institute. Three years of hell. For now, I was stuck in Holmesburg – a hundred year old, dilapidated, smelly, old hell hole. I did not know what to expect in Graterford. More of the same?

I had not made a misstep growing up. Well, hardly any. My parents had done well and I was sent to a fine private school. I was one of three Jews in the school, but I had been a good football player and had no problems. Well, hardly any. These old line white bread institutions had many unspoken rules. The English love rules, especially hidden ones that have to be ingrained from birth. I had to learn the rules.

First rule: Dress appropriately. The old line WASPs were uncanny in their way to scan your clothing for the proper color, the proper stitching, the proper line, the proper cut. The merest deviation would be sorted out, and you would be exposed as a fraud. I have to thank my mother for this one. She figured out where all the kids got their clothes.

It was Jacob Reeds. A store for kids with the proper Ivy League look – the basic blue oxford button down shirt with the exact length of the collars, and the exact oxford weave. Khakis almost always a light tan, but sometimes a permissible black, never blue or brown, never a grey unless it was wool flannel. The shoes were brown penny loafers – never black, never mahogany, but brown, dark brown. Socks – off white wool socks – never white, never cotton.

We had to wear coats and ties every day. Usually the blue blazer with the school patch on the pocket and the school tie. Often a tweed jacket was okay, but the proper tweed was a problem – it had to have the correct colors and pattern – the safest was a one color – often brown or tan – herring bone patterns. Ties could be striped but of course only approved English colors – regimental and school colors with the proper stripe widths were acceptable. Deviations were not.

The "Ivy League" indoctrination took months and had a few mishaps along the way. But mom was resilient and caught on fast. In a year, I had the correct wardrobe.

Manners were another thing. Not just please and thank you, but a myriad of other conventions. Older people were always "Sir" or "Ma'am" or a full Mr. or Mrs. – no uncles or aunts. I was also surprised shabbiness was "in." You couldn't look too rich and your clothes or your car could be old – even shabby and beat up. Shoes could be cracked, shirt collars could be frayed, even ties could be frayed. A new shiny car was not well received unless it was a "woody" station wagon, or a small but inexpensive sports car – a proper Ford – not usually a Chevy – four door was acceptable, but an oldie, well worn.

No women worked, or had maids. Men washed their own cars, mowed their lawns and did their own painting – even if they could afford it. The men constantly repeated variations of the Protestant work ethic.

The arts were out unless it was classical music. Ballet, oil painting, whether impressionist or expressionist, modern novels, poetry of any sort. French or Italian things were deemed a bit too emotional or sexual. The arts were replaced by sports – and only some sports – baseball and football were prime, basketball was a bit lower class, tennis was okay, golf was for the newly rich, for girls: hockey, lacrosse and tennis. And sports over learning – a good athlete was admired throughout his lifetime if his stardom only occurred in high school. Brilliant students, achievers in the worlds of business, law, medicine research were never recognized at alumni functions. Awards for every conceivable athletic achievement were plentiful; for academics – sparse and limited and known only to the inner circle.

It was a continuous exercise to figure out the not usually intuitive convention.

The next was religion. While the school advertised itself as nonsectarian, it had a magnificent old chapel with handsome stain glass windows. Four times a week there was "chapel," in which traditional English and German Protestant hymns were sung, and "sermons" along with readings from the *New Testament*. I learned about 40 different hymns including the school hymn in which we asserted that "Christ is the strength and Christ the might." Needless to say for a Jewish boy, this was disconcerting. What was I supposed to do when I had to say "Jesus" or "Christ?" Was anyone looking when I didn't sing the hymns?

At the same time, I was going to Hebrew school to prepare for my bar mitzvah. The religious stories were in total conflict. But only in my mind. No one knew of my Wednesdays off for Hebrew school except that I missed football practice. Since I was now the starting quarterback, this took some explaining by the coach – who also taught eighth grade. He was cool about it. After my bar mitzvah, the rest of the season I was there.

Another issue was my brain. I was of course anxious to fit in, but smart kids were often marginalized as "too brainy." Of course, I had my smart friends, but for the rest of the class, I didn't want to appear smart. I was able to early claim the moniker of class clown, which earned me a few disciplinary actions which I wore as a badge of honor. I have to say that, except for a few minor exceptions, I suffered no embarrassing incidents of prejudice. In fact, my years at Oak Tree Academy were happy and successful. All my efforts at assimilation were mainly in my own head. I have to say that this WASP world was tolerant, educated and totally accepting.

College was even better. Although at Yale, there was the perpetual one-third of "preppies" – members of wealthy families, with great connections who had gone to upper crust boarding schools, and were guaranteed a walk into the freshman class; the rest of the school was intellectually superior. The preppies usually stuck to themselves, were well aware of the easy courses and majors, and took them. They clustered in three exclusive fraternities and were never heard from. The rest of us were like young lords on Olympus – everything was excellent – courses, professors, even sports, dramatics, the newspaper, everything. We could take pride in everything. We did. It was a wonderful sheltered world where we could develop and learn to think.

Law school has a very limited peek at the outside world. It was wonderful in the way it required students to be prepared every day to argue with the professor and fellow students about the law. Since I went to Villanova Law School, I found it refreshing every day that the classrooms were directly across the street from the seminary and we could see novitiates walking around the campus in their brown robes. It was also refreshing that the law students and novitiates could get into their gym clothes and play basketball on the seminary court. Law school was also a mixture of students from all levels of the socio-economic hierarchy, all religions, and all attitudes. We somehow felt we would greatly influence the politics of the next generation. But mainly, we studied, and were berated regularly by our professors to toughen us up to the contradictions of the outside world.

One of the most illuminating moments in law school came during an intense argument between a law professor and several of the students. In analyzing a case, the class believed that the court in its opinion had reached a particularly harsh and unfair result. We insisted it was unjust. The professor, a hard bitten intense old fellow, grinned as if he had made his point. Pointing to the monks across the street in their brown robes and cowls, "You want 'fair,' go across the street. Here we teach law."

It was a great relief that after law school, I was now an adult and had been offered a well-paying job with a prestigious law firm, Dunstan, Charter & Fisk. Was I there yet? So far no mistakes, hard work. I was on the right path.

The law firm was a strange new world. We were required of course to wear a suit and tie every day. The shirt could be either white or blue – never striped, never yellow or pink unless you were one of the superior rain makers – men who brought in large clients who paid humungous fees. We were to wear our suit jackets any time we left our individual offices, never in the hallways; we were never to loosen our ties – ever, or walk with our hands in our pockets.

There was a strict hierarchy. Senior partners ran the firm. Junior partners had little say in what happened in the firm, but got a percentage of the profits. Senior associates handled very complex matters and occasionally saw the clients, and junior associates were worked to death – 70 to 80 hours a week, often Saturdays and sometimes Sundays. We did the most menial tasks – getting coffee, proofreading, walking clients' dogs but mainly research and producing memoranda on troubling points of law that arose for the partners.

The new associates were assigned to work in various departments. Every law student pictures himself as a famous trial lawyer. I was no exception. I of course wanted litigation – the trial department. I was assigned to real estate – one of the most boring, stultifying, detail oriented parts. One thing most young lawyers don't understand is that trial work doesn't make money. It eats up hours, is never profitable and is very unpredictable. Facts and legal arguments arise that were never expected or intended. Witnesses lie, wimp out, forget, or are just plain stupid. Judges can come up with total misreadings of the case. In short, a law firm can ill afford to try a case where a good client is involved, especially if it is a personal matter – divorce, a business dissolution, a partnership dispute, even the minor matters of their children. As a result they paper the case to death – file irrelevant motions, waste time, postpone delay, then settle. Settle for whatever makes the client the least unhappy. Unfortunately this consumes hours of lawyer time which is billable. Often, billable hours must be written off to satisfy a good corporate client. I did not know it, but the firm in assigning me to real estate was doing me a favor – I was in the safest place for a long happy career. Unlike litigation, real estate almost always involved big bucks, and justified big fees. Also, it involved large heavy piles of documents. True. But most of the language came from prior deals and those awesome wads of paper were merely plagiarized, i.e. cut and pasted, from past transactions. So the hours billed were far more than the hours actually expended. There was far less stress. Only long boring hours proofreading documents and looking pompous and pedantic in front of your clients and opposing lawyers. So real estate it was.

The sad part was that real estate was the area least capable of inventive thought. Creativity was a sin, because it raised possible issues in multi-million dollar deals no one wanted to test. Protect the client and make the deal go through. Don't be a hero. Just do your job, become a pillar in the community, join a country club and send your kids to private school.

So I bought into it. My senior associate was a dull guy who knew how to protect his position, i.e. cover his ass. He had been an editor of a law review and delighted in giving me research assignments and then finding fault with my grammar, writing style and having me re-write the item. I suppose he thought he was mentoring me, but it did little for my evaluation in the firm. Hours spent profitably, i.e. capable of being billed to the client, are a measure of an associate's performance. Since very few of my hours were actually billed, my senior associates did me little benefit. Since most of my work was what my senior associates considered "remedial writing," I got precious little credit for my time. I also noticed that few of my suggestions of the law got included in the file, but were included in the senior associates' letters to the client, signed by the senior partner. Ah! Such is life in the law firm world. Since my other junior associate buddies complained about the same thing, I wrote it off to standard practice.

But I did make two mistakes. In my second year, I got a client, a good one. One of my friends from growing up was the son of a real estate developer who built a number of homes each year. Another large firm did the work for his father. The son, wisely, decided he wanted his own trusted counsel and I was it. He persuaded his father to let me do all the settlements on the homes they sold – a simple enough, repetitive job that required me to spend one day of week out of the office. It was not a great pay day but it demonstrated my ability to attract business – a vital concern for law firms, not usually demonstrated until the associate was much further along. I also got a handsome percentage of the fee which put me in net pay above my senior associate, Ivan Gardner, who had not yet managed to attract a client, but was reliable in satisfying the concerns of existing clients. But he would never be a rainmaker – a partner who attracted new clients. He was a dull guy with few social skills and bad hygiene. He spoke in a low mumble, still had some teenage acne, and was always digging in his ears, often with a paperclip. While he did not have bad breath, he had a heavy odor about him which was accentuated when he had to complete a large real estate settlement. But he was reliable, and could tend capably to the affairs of large existing clients. I could feel him rumble as he handed me my bonus check for my client's closings. That was a stat all the firm could see.

The next mistake was opening my big mouth. We, as a firm, represented some of the big entities in the city – a major utility, one of the big banks, a university, a hospital and medical school, one of the private schools. In a way, the bigger firms divided up the big entities with big legal billings among themselves to avoid conflicts of interest. When some large transaction would occur, it was an occasion for all the senior partners involved to appear while the senior associates did all the work and the junior associates hustled in and out running errands. It created the appearance of a full service firm, and implied that the entity could never go with a smaller firm.

This occasion was a municipal bond closing. The federal government favors our cities by letting them finance its activities and issue bonds paying interest, but the interest on those bonds is tax free to investors. Wealthy investors can buy these bonds and receive, let's say, five percent interest tax free which can be the equivalent of buying eight percent bonds from for-profit corporations. The cities then save large amounts in interest payments and get to build hospitals, sewers, bridges, etc. for far less in monthly payments. Most of these city agencies are in small Republican controlled parts of our state, and most states, so the work and the profits on these deals go to well-connected Republican sources.

Republican law firms cultivate assiduously these small Republican towns and their politicians for bond work. Now, the bond work is easy. It is often repetitive boilerplate in massive quantities that has been used in multiple previous transactions. Since the fee is often a percentage of the dollars involved in the transaction, no one checks the actual hours spent in preparing what looks like cartons and cartons of paperwork, but is in fact spit out of computers with minor changes from the previous transaction. In this way, barely educated politicians reward the law firm and the lead stock brokerage firm that places the bonds, and they in turn fund their political campaigns, if not quite a few other activities. Also, in this way, the law firms hire hack Republican politicians to cultivate these backwoods Republicans for their work. The big firms are also expected to pay local firms for non-existent work on long forms. Principal bond work is a very lucrative and closely guarded domain of the big firms.

Regularly, the firm would put on a dog and pony show for the bond closing. The politicians from the small municipalities, and their lawyers, were brought into Philadelphia, wined and dined, or possibly more depending on moral proclivities. They were then ushered into an immense paneled boardroom.

The dark paneling in the board room was handsomely accented with oil paintings of former ex-partners, exquisite landscapes of Philadelphia, and huge plate glass windows looking out on the Port of Philadelphia from the upper floor of our high rise office building. In addition to upstate politicians and their lawyers, there were the representatives of the stock brokerage firm and their lawyers. Everyone's lawyers had to check over the work our firm did in preparation for closing and then we had to go through a lengthy signing process and fax documents all over. Then money from the brokerage firms would be wired into our firm's account, who then would dispense it to everyone. It was an all-day affair in which people mainly sat around and chatted. The actual legal work was relatively small, the fees huge.

This time the Borough of Cataclump in Wessex County needed a medical center – basically a primary care health clinic which could feed major medical cases out to the larger hospitals in Scranton. The mayor, his rather attractive secretary, his council president and a lawyer from a small firm in Cataclump were ushered into the boardroom. They had spent the night in our local five star hotel and been wined and dined by our senior partner who also was the head of the Republican Party in Philadelphia County. It was interesting that our senior partner had never won an election himself, nor did Philadelphia have a single elected republican office holder. In fact Republican registration in Philadelphia was less than 20 percent. But he had the "old boy" connections in the statewide Republican organizations to generate the clout for numerous municipal bond financings per year and was handsomely rewarded even though he would not know a municipal bond prospect if it bit him in the ass.

The financing had the not particularly unusual wrinkle that the bonds were secured by a mortgage on the land where the medical center and its parking lot would be built. Thus, the real estate department was brought in to be sure the mortgage was properly prepared and placed of record after the closing. Our department prepared and filed numerous mortgages each year and this one was not particularly unique, except that it defined land carved out of a parcel the mayor and his lawyer owned near the highway in

Cataclump. So we had to check the survey. Big deal! No problems! Good deal for the mayor and the lawyer. Very good.

As the Cataclump people walked in, they huddled together and seemed intimidated by our receptionist with the fake BBC English accent, our thick oriental rugs in front of the immense empty receptionist desk, and the four units of armor standing at attention in the corners. The Cataclumpians were dressed in a variety of fashions. The mayor had his best blue suit from Sears, an orange dress shirt, and light tan wing tip shoes. His secretary, about 35-ish and attractive, was wearing a mini-skirt and low cut blouse, the attorney wore a plaid sports coat, khakis and black hush pie's. They were grateful for the coffee. They would spend the day in the conference room only to spend less than a minute signing papers. We had only expected two guests from Cataclump since we only needed two signatures. The mayor, Eugene Wachiewicz – was a local realtor in his late 50s, Salvatore Pernicio was the owner of the local saw mill. Both held their elective positions on a part-time basis. The secretary, Denise Diamond, was unexpected but added on by the mayor "to collate papers," but we surmised she had important functions under the mayor. Lawyers are used to client confidentiality and this occasion was not to be an exception.

The brokerage boys came in. They were dressed in high fashion with boldly striped shirts and contrasting suits with wide heavy silk ties. Tasseled black loafers were de rigueur. But they were waiting for their attorney.

We began without their attorney since there was a good deal of paper shuffling, and initialing to do. When he eventually showed he had a worried look on his face. Opening his brief case, he said, "Gentlemen, we have a problem."

With that, I could feel the collective blood pressure rise and the collective body odor permeate the room.

"One of the bond buyers had to back out. They didn't have the cash, and their independent appraiser did not think the center would generate the income necessary for the bond's payments." Now, you must understand that, for all his depressed demeanor, the brokers boys' attorney took no small pleasure in the announcement. This deal had been in the works for weeks, and, if there had been any problems, they should have been raised by the appraiser long before. But the lawyer was from a competing firm and was using its representation of the brokerage firm to discredit our firm in front of our clients. He was like the witch who showed up at Sleeping Beauty's birthday party and condemned her to death. All at once, our firm crumbled. The partner who was the Republican politician sat stunned, the tax partner gasped, the securities partner put his head in his hands, the senior associate for real estate began to pick his nose nervously, our secretaries were like deer frozen in the headlights, and each junior associate looked around to their bosses for answers. A number of voices broke out at once.

"Ed, why didn't you tell us before."

"Who's the appraiser. Ours had no problem."

"Where is this appraiser, who the hell is he, who does he think he is."

"Does this mean the deal is dead."

"Who'll pay our fees?"

"Does this mean the land can't be sold?"

In the meantime, I sat down to look at the survey and our own appraisal. Our appraisal included parts of the adjoining counties in the area from which our medical center would grow. The brokerage firm's appraisal had not – a stupid mistake. He used only the immediate county's residents.

"Ed, why didn't we hear about this earlier?"

"I sent it over a few days ago."

"To whom?" The senior partner for corporate matters glared around at all of the members of our firm in the conference room. Heads could roll.

"Well, let me get the transmittal letter... Here, it is. Ah, I see the problem. We sent it to the wrong floor."

At this, a large shouting match broke out. Our firm lost huge fees, the big bank lost its fees, Cataclump lost its medical center and the brokerage firm lost its fees. Most of all the mayor and his lawyer lost their bond sale. Suits were threatened. A verbal melee of global proportions ensued.

Meanwhile, I picked up the brokerage firms survey and read it over quickly. Our plan was for an 80,000 square foot medical center which costs $9,000,000 in total and the appraisal came in at a valuation projection of $7,500.000. So we were $1,500,000 short. It would take weeks to redo the appraisal and reassemble the closing for a new bond financing. Interest rates could change. The market could dry up. This certainly would kill the deal.

Okay, so we would need another $1,500,000, we couldn't go the municipal bond route, but we needed to finance 20,000 feet and fast. So I started doing some numbers in my head.

An idea popped up. This medical center was to be one story for 80,000 square feet. But if we added a second story for doctors' offices, a pharmacy, and some other medically related functions – physical therapy, nursing home beds, we might be able to fill up another 60,000 feet at least on the second floor. We would have to buy $1,500,000 and take rights to the second floor. We could then get a private mortgage for the additional 20,000 feet on the first floor plus 40,000 feet on the second floor. The problem was that we couldn't build it all at once. The second phase would have to go later, but provisions had to be made for it. This presented a second problem. How to redesign the center for a second story after the first story was already built? I had a buddy, Joel Arnstein, who was a junior associate at an architectural firm in town. I called him and explained the problem and explained the situation in our conference room. He could hear the din of arguments in the background. He chuckled.

"Don't worry. It's easy peasy. Just sink some more footers, what we call pilasters, about three feet as you're building the first stage and then you construct the second stage on top when you're ready."

"What would these pilasters cost?"

"You say for 60,000 square feet?" I could hear him breathing as he worked out the numbers on his calculator.

"Somewhere between $50,000 and $100,000 give or take depending on the soil and the bedrock."

"If I sent you the plans, how soon could you redo them to show the pilasters, the utilities, etc."

"Maybe a day or two."

"Could you go to Cataclump to oversee the work, and authorize the progress payouts?"

"No sweat."

"Great. Hold on, I'll call you back."

So now we had enough to build 60,000 square feet on the second floor. Or total rentable space of another 60,000 feet. Could this be worth the $1,500,000 we needed? Could we sell this off? I did some more numbers. At $15 per square foot, rental value, with construction costs at $70 per square foot. It would cost $4.2 million in construction, $1.5 million for the 60,000 square feet or a total of $5.7 million – call it $6 million with contingencies. This would generate $900,000 per year in income or a 15 percent return – very nice. We could get a mortgage for $6.0 million and not pay another penny. The bank would lend us 80% of the additional $1.5 million in municipal bonds. We would need $300,000 to make the deal work.

I thought I had it done, so I called on the senior partner and interrupted him in the midst of a tirade against Ed. "Mr. Tinker, sir. I think I have a solution. Would you hear me out?" This was a tremendous breach of protocol – a junior associate interrupting the senior partner in front of an assembled multitude of assorted entities. When Mr. Tinker turned to me, he said, "This better be good."

With great trepidation and knowing my career was on the line, I walked over to the easel in the corner and picked up a magic marker and explained my reasoning and put up the numbers. I added in the results of my call to Joel about the pilasters. After speaking for about a half hour, and calculating the numbers, I said, "So basically, the 20,000 on the first floor and the 60,000 on the second has to be worth more than $1.5 million. So if we reserve this out of the plan, we can sell it off to raise the rest of the money."

The brokerage firm's attorney was the first to ask, "How do you reserve this out?"

"We create a commercial condominium and separate it out in a deed of condominium."

"How do we redraw the plans to accommodate the pilasters and the description of the second phase?"

"My friend, Joel Arnstein, said he could do it in a few days and be available to supervise the construction if need be."

"I can see that this investment of $1.5 million saves the project, and would generate a nice income, but who is going to buy it. It is a very complicated scheme and would be hard to sell."

"Your firm, my firm and the mayor and his lawyer will."

"What?" This came from about six to eight people at once.

"Okay. The mayor and his lawyer are selling their land for $800,000 if the deal goes through. The brokerage firm makes about $150,000, and our firm gets $80,000 in fees if the deed goes through. The bank gets $300,000. That is if we pay in cash into an escrow fund. If the bank is willing to lend 50 percent on the investment in consideration of it getting the fees from the construction loans and the management of the bond payout over 30 years. We have our $1,500,000. If we don't do this, the deal is dead and all the fees die with it. If all goes well and we put our money into escrow, we end up as partners in a deal for $1,500,000 which yields about $385,000 per year."

The room was quiet. I could feel the lawyers from my firm back away from me as if I had the plague. My senior associate wanted to bore a hole through me with his glare. I had broken many basic rules: Don't show up the senior partner. Don't show up your senior associate. But also – the firm never gets into business deals with clients, the firm never takes risky fees on future contingencies, the firm avoids conflicts of interest at all costs. Eventually, each of the parties huddled up and got on their cell phones. I sat alone at one end of the conference room, as if I just broken wind.

The bank's lawyer spoke up. "How soon could we redo the papers and have a second closing?" This was not directed at me but at the senior partner, who looked at the senior associate.

He was aghast. Could they seriously be considering this preposterous idea and… for a junior associate? But the senior partner wanted an answer. "I guess a few days."

"Good," was all the senior partner said.

The huddles reassembled.

Finally, the brokerage firm's attorney spoke up. "We believe we would go along with this if it can be done by the end of next week." Those knowledgeable people in the room knew he was taking a big risk. They had about five or six other brokerage firms involved in the deal and would have to convince them of the merits of the new arrangement or buy the bonds themselves. That they were willing to participate in the risk was a huge endorsement. The mayor and his lawyer, knowing they were making a huge profit on the sale of the property, were willing to play with the house's money and go along with the deal or lose it. The bank's lawyer was skeptical still and looked to our senior partner. After all, our firm also represented the bank and relied on us for this kind of advice. The senior partner was now forced to make a choice between breaking the rules of our firm or losing face by killing the deal over $80,000. With his balls in a vise, he agreed but was not happy.

People in the room were starting to get up and leave as the lunch order from the nearby deli was being delivered. The meeting was over and no one wanted to sit at the table and eat lunch while trying to make pleasant conversation when they were in such a state of turmoil. No one was particularly happy because they came in expecting a routine closing ceremony and now had a cobbled together deal they did not really understand. I had opened my big mouth, saved everyone's ass and was still a pariah.

Fortunately, there were no more glitches. Joel redid the blueprints and defined the areas to be split off into two separate condominiums. I drew up the condominium documents, the limited partnership documents for new 60,000 foot space and redid some of the bond financing documents. The brokerage house re-sold the municipal bonds based on the new prospectus. The bank approved the loan for $750,000 for the 60,000 square foot area. All the people involved in the new space signed up for the limited partnership interests. The only one that raised an objection was my firm. They felt that they had problems investing along with clients and taking a piece of the action. I offered to take the firm's place in the deal and it was approved. Joel got the business of supervising the construction.

Closing went through smoothly with all the participants showing up the following Friday. We were told that the appraiser whose work screwed up the prior settlement was told to limit his projected area to the county by the brokerage firm who denied it. I never heard the end of that story.

After closing, as a new member of the limited partnership owning the new 60,000 area, I got on the phone with CVS real estate guy whom I had met at a previous closing. I explained the deal, sent him the prospectus and the blue prints. He immediately agreed to locate an 18,000 square foot pharmacy in the complex at $15 a square foot. He was going to forward his proposal out the next day.

We had dodged a bullet and came out very nicely. Yet, I could still hear some negative rumblings in the firm. I had embarrassed some key people.

I think the most galling aspect of the transaction to all the others but especially my firm was that I had been creative. In law, creativity is viewed with great skepticism. It smacks of unreliability. Most corporate lawyers are hide bound, uncreative, compulsive, over achievers. They rely on prior precedent and only feel comfortable in control of everything. I had demonstrated I was not of that mold. I was the black sheep. I scared them. The law at the top was not a creative institution.

GRATERFORD S.C.I.

Graterford S.C.I. was another of Pennsylvania's overcrowded, ancient lockups where I was to spend my next three years. The guard banged on my cell at 5:00 a.m. and I collected my few belongings and was led out to a room by the gate, where I sat and sat. A female guard came by and handed me a box lunch of bologna sandwich and an orange, with a paraffin container of some kind of orange drink. I guessed this was my lunch. I ate and sat some more. About three hours later, the van for Graterford came and I went on with three other prisoners. We were handcuffed to the floor and locked into leg irons. The trip through the city, out the expressway and onto 422 to the Collegeville exit was uneventful. I envisioned briefly a Harrison Ford escape as in "The Fugitive," but I was only serving three years and would be out in my early 30s. Besides, I wanted to prove I was not guilty and I needed help.

A bunch of surly guards tried to intimidate us, shoved clothes at us and in a sing song recited the rules. I guess they had seen too many Tommy John movies. I was processed into a cell, and processed another bologna sandwich box lunch because we had arrived too late for lunch.

I was directed to a cell block and had my door opened. Inside was an older black man leaning back on a chair in the cell reading a paperbound. I nodded hello and asked him which bed he wanted.

"Call me Satchel, like Satchel Page. How you doing?"

"Not too bad."

"Since you're younger, you get the top bunk. I ain't as spry as I used to be. What are you in for?" Probably everyone's first question.

"Embezzlement."

15

"How long you in for?"

"Three years min."

"Embezzlement, huh? Did they find the money?"

"No."

"Huh! Three years for how much?"

"Three million dollars."

"Sweet deal, I'd do that."

"Well, I'm innocent. I didn't get the money."

"Sure, sure. Everyone says that. I get it. I ain't no jailhouse snitch, but other guys are gonna get real close to you."

"I guessed that."

"So what did you do before?"

"I was a lawyer."

"Wow, a criminal lawyer?"

"No. Real estate."

"Uh-huh. Well, don't say that. Just say lawyer. You are gonna be real popular real soon. Guys are gonna have you look into their cases."

"I'm not real interested in that."

"Well, you better be, because in here you need something to protect you. There's guys that want to get to you somehow some way. You know what I mean?"

"So, I've heard."

"Well, if you are helping some with their cases, they help you. You got it?"

"Got it. Now, Satchel, I'm real tired and I need some sleep and time to think. Can we talk about this later?"

"Sure. Sure. But wow, I got me a lawyer for a cellie. I'm gonna be in hog heaven. Anything you want, you just ask."

"Great, Satchel. Thanks." I rolled over in my bed and tried to nap, but images kept pouring into my head, negative ones, now. I was getting bouts of anxiety and depression coming on, I could feel it. Somehow, I drifted off to sleep, but couldn't escape the recent events.

First Dinner at Graterford

Satchel, also known as Rigby Hayes, woke me just before dinner.

"Thanks, Satchel. I didn't want to miss dinner."

"You don't know that yet. Don't be too quick to say that."

"Anyway, Satchel, what are you in for?"

"A holdup. I was 31 and I stuck up a grocery store. Got $123 and 30 years."

"Thirty years! Why so much?"

"One of my guys shot a customer on the way out. He died, so felony murder?"

"Did you have a gun?"

"Yep. Sure did."

"Can't you get parole, I must be 10 years by now."

"I been up for parole lots of times, but I max out this fall in October."

"Well that's great."

"Yes and no. I don't know where to go or what to do."

"How 'bout a halfway house."

"I missed out on that. I'm rated violent."

"When the next hearing?"

"Next week."

"Let me see if I can help you. I haven't been disbarred yet. What do you want? Halfway house, parole."

"I have two sisters left in Philadelphia, so I think a halfway house there."

"I could get you a job, I think. What can you do?"

"Oh, I was a bartender. I had been at the Ritz Carlton for five years. You should see me in one of those spiffy uniforms. I can also cook."

"Ok, a halfway house and a bartending job. Let's work on that."

By this time, we got to the dining hall and I sat with Satchel and his buddies. The dinner wasn't too bad – mystery meat in gravy, mashed potatoes, and some overcooked string beans. Satchel and his buddies were all older cons, in their 50s and 60s, ignored by the rest of the population. They talked about old times, and the Eagles. Satchel of course bragged that his cellie was a lawyer.

The hall was large and noisy. We sat at wooden picnic tables. Some of the young guys talked in loud voices. I could not make out too much, they used black prison slang and heavy black accents. It is noticeable that when a group is oppressed they develop their own language.

There were several distinct groups in the mess hall. The Muslims controlled several tables in one corner. The Muslim culture seemed to be attractive to young black males who were raised with little discipline because it imposed a strong regiment of prayer, fasting, obedience and ritual. Either something in the human spirit craved this structure and discipline or the men joined the Muslim group for protection in prison. I have always wondered whether this was a good thing or not. Did they join Muslim criminal gangs when they got out, or pursue the strict moral codes? Someone will have to do a study. Generally, the Muslims left you alone if you left them alone. Fine with me.

Other gangs large and small clustered together for mutual protection. Satchel and his crew were no exception. I had no desire to join the white group, so Satchel and his buddies felt comfortable.

After dinner, I could feel my euphoria over my freedom from the law firm and my fiancée fade, and the beginnings of anxiety and depression sink in. I began to dwell on the facts of my case, my arrest and my trial. I couldn't sleep and didn't eat much. I could see I was in a downward spiral. I barely mumbled to Satchel and staggered through the prison schedule of meals and counts and inspections in a withdrawn passive state.

In Jail at 3:00 A.M.
After Trial

I awoke again at what seemed in the dark of night still in Holmesburg. Since they took everything from me but a pile of prison jump suits and my own sneakers, socks and underwear, I had no wrist watch. Or of course, any books yet. I would never have the Internet, or my own phone. I guessed I had been asleep about four or five hours because I had to pee. I rolled off the lower bunk and urinated in the commode in the dark. Since the commode had no toilet seat, I hoped I was not spraying on the upper rim or on the floor. My cellmate snored peacefully beside me. He was a petty drug dealer from Chester who would remain in this jail until he had served his six months minimum sentence. He was a nice enough Hispanic man in his fifties and had offered me the lower bunk. I would be picked up from this Holmesburg Prison sometime early in the morning and taken to Graterford about 45 minutes away. I had been sent to Holmesburg immediately after sentencing the previous day. The best way to describe Holmesburg is a dog kennel. The walls are mostly old field stone from the late 1800s, the cell was about six feet by nine feet and house at least two prisoners. Sometimes a third sleeps on the floor on a foam rubber matt. The windows have old fashioned cross hatch bars, and the door and front wall are all steel bars with a door in the middle. We are totally observable to the guards on patrol. I believe I was put with this cellmate because he was older and not inclined to violence. Maybe, they were being kind, maybe they didn't want to write up any trouble or maybe it was just luck. I couldn't complain about him.

As I lay on my back trying to fall back to sleep, I was forced to review my life – something prison time amply affords. My mind drifted to my fiancée – Bonnie Rosenberg. It had only been a matter of time before she stopped seeing me after the arrest. I have to admit, I felt a kind of relief. In fact, I had a vague sense that my life had not suffered a catastrophe as much as another spin of the wheel. The tension and stress from my work was leaving me as I realized I had no job, no money and didn't have to answer to anyone. I would be a clean slate.

Considering that I was entirely innocent of the charges counter balanced that feeling. I did feel anger and a desire for vindication and revenge, but that would come. Somehow I felt that that would come.

I remembered my fiancée. Bonnie Rosenberg was a different story. She was a nice girl from an upper middle class family. She had the smarts to go to the University of Pennsylvania. From seventh grade on, she had been among the popular girls and, at Penn, she was in the premier Jewish sorority which dated the premier Jewish fraternity. The two houses were attractive, had nice meals, were respectable and sought after. They had several formals each year, and had stand up cocktail parties after football games. They were all well-dressed. Most of the men went to Wharton – the famous Penn business school which rivaled Harvard, but was more focused and practical, less theoretical. Bonnie was a beautiful girl with shiny black hair, dark eyebrows and large brown eyes. Her years of dance training gave her a superb figure, and she could model the latest fashion on a par with anyone in her sorority. She was great arm candy.

But I was a catch. A lawyer in a prestigious firm on the way up. I was definitely a first round draft choice in the husband category. While not very big, I was a pretty good athlete but in a sport no one knew or appreciated – wrestling. I was leaner, meaner, more fit and more athletic than most of the other Penn fraternity, but no one cared. Except Bonnie she knew little about sports, but did come to the wrestling meets with me and sometimes came to the gym to work out with me. She did mainly stretching and ballet moves, and wore the latest gym fashions. At the gym, guys are never fashionable so she would cluck at me if I was seen outside in my ragged tank top and worn shorts.

Her parents invited me to the country club for dinner. Her father was a very decent guy who sold mostly meat and deli products and had by dint of hard work and hustle made himself successful. Her mother was totally decked out – her reddish hair had blond streaks, gold jewelry on wrists, ears and neck, and a designer dress. She wanted to know who my parents were, and quizzed me about our relatives. I felt like I was being processed. She did not check my teeth, however.

Of course, it did not take long after my arrest for Bonnie to break up and return my ring. Since the feds were sure to look for it, I hid it in a nice place. I can't say I blame Bonnie. She had been trained to look for certain roles, and being a tragic heroine was not one of them. She would have been a good mother, kept an immaculate house, been a fine hostess, could have even appeared on stage as a political candidate's wife, worked diligently for a host of charities. But the arrest was an acid test, and she was gone. I understood. By the way the sex was not bad. As she faded from view, I drifted back to sleep.

Arrest and Trial

But from there to jail. How did all this happen?

I had to linger on the arrest and trial: a gruesome nightmare that attacked me in the daytime as well.

I remembered I was sitting at my desk putting together a shopping center lease for one of our clients. These are long tedious documents that run on for pages and cover contingencies that rarely occur but show the lawyer was going to great extremes protecting his client and accumulating reams of paper to prove it.

Joanne, the secretary that several associates shared came in and, in voice which was trembling, said "Some men are here to see you." Already, a number of people had gathered in the hallway outside my door. They must have known what was to follow.

Three men in FBI windbreakers and a Philadelphia cop stood at my doorway. "Mr. Jacobson, could you please come with us?"

"What's going on?"

"Mr. Jacobson, you are under arrest. Please come into the hallway." One of the men had his hand on a gun at his waist.

I rose and came to the door. They spun me around and put metal handcuffs on me, very tight, and began to read me my rights. The one reading off the card was almost chuckling in a smarmy sort of way when they got to the part about the right to a lawyer. The FBI has a disdain for lawyers, especially big firm, corporate types, although they usually see the low rent, criminal defense lawyers.

I tried to speak to ask what this was about. I was told to shut up and walk. In my "perp walk," I noticed practically the entire firm, including paralegals and secretaries, had come out to the hallway to watch my arrest. The senior partners were standing in the lobby as I kept asking what I had done. I was pushed into a car into the bottom floor of the building after running another gauntlet of curious people. Once in the squad car, the siren and lights were turned on as I went down to the "roundhouse" – the police administration building with holding cells in the basement where prisoners were kept pending their preliminary arraignment. First they took my fingerprints and a photo and then, my wallet, belt and shoe laces. I was marched down to a cell. They told me they that this would take 10 to 22 hours for them to "process me," before I could get bail.

Roundhouse, Arraignment, Lawyer

I recalled surviving my time in the cell in the basement of the Round House before being called to a spare courtroom on the first floor. I had called to a friend of mine from law school to come to my preliminary arraignment. This, I knew, from law school was a short hearing to set my bail. I had already filled out a form giving my "ties to the community" – a key factor in granting low or no bail. I had a job, parents in the area, a sister in the area, a fiancé in the area, I had a law degree and was admitted to the Pennsylvania and Federal Bar. My crime apparently was embezzlement – that was all I knew so far. The "processing" involved the court people – of whom there were few after 5:00 p.m. checking out my statements. After running my fingerprints through the computer and checking out my assertions on my bail – worthiness, I was finally called up the next day to the courtroom at 9:00 a.m. The previous judge had gone home at 4:00 a.m. and decided not to take any more cases although 14 of us remained below.

When I came upstairs, the lawyer I had called had not yet checked in, so the public defender stepped in. He handed me a few pieces of paper – a copy of the form I had filled out with comments by the bail processors and a charge sheet which gave me for the first time a few details about my alleged crime. It seems I embezzled $3,100,000 from the law firm of Dunstan, Charter & Fisk. This was the first I had heard of it. The prosecutor read out the charge to the judge and then commented that I appeared to have enough to flee the country and therefore, should be incarcerated until trial, but he would agree to $300,000 bail – a sum I did not have. The public defender whispered that I would only need $30,000 to get out. I told him I was innocent of the charges, and had no desire to run, I had a promising legal career here and wasn't fleeing anywhere. He made the appropriate remarks to the judge. The judge who now had 28 more cases backed up to hear, granted me "ROR" or allowed me to sign my own bail papers for $50,000 and walk free. He handed me an order. I was then directed to my shoe laces, belt and whatever else they had taken from me earlier. I was sure to note the name of the prosecutor who wanted me incarcerated until trial – an unkempt young man in an ill-fitting suit, and scuffed loafers named Cianci. I called the lawyer I had asked to come to the roundhouse and told him I didn't need him. He was still not in his office as yet. I walked out to the Chinatown area which was directly next to the roundhouse, I went back to my apartment. On the papers I was given, I was told that I had a preliminary hearing in 10 days at the police station at 21st and Winter Streets. I called the office and asked Joanne if I had any messages. She could only say the head of the real estate department wanted to see me the next day and I was not expected back in until then. I went back to my apartment and took a long nap.

It was noon when I woke up. There were things that had to be done. First, I needed a decent criminal lawyer but who? Then, I needed to find out what they were saying I had done and review the evidence. Then I had to answer all the calls. I finally came in to see the senior real estate partner and tried to explain.

"But I didn't do this. I would never have known how to do this. I didn't do bond work."

"I'm sure you'll have your day in court. But until then, I'm sorry."

I could feel the blood drawn from my head, I felt faint. I could feel my stomach rumble. There was nothing more to say. All my efforts in law school and with the firm were down the drain. I just got up and walked out. No other words were necessary. Somehow, someway, I was set up.

Planning a Defense

As I walked back to my apartment, ideas began to flash in my head. I needed a criminal defense lawyer, and we had to start investigating right away. From what the senior partner said there was documentary evidence to look at. And my money. I realized that if they proved I had stolen something, they would take my money. I had to pay a lawyer and I had to hide my money. The 401(k) contributions were probably at risk. My stocks were still mine and so was my condo. I had to figure out a way to sell it. There was no way I could protect my investment in the Cataclump hospital site – all my brilliant effort could be a loss.

So get the money out and pay a lawyer first. I interviewed a few of the more prominent ones, but was disappointed when I tried to explain the commercial transactions that were involved. Very few criminal defense lawyers practice what is called "white collar" crime and very few have any familiarity with commercial transactions. No. I was going to have to go to one of the more expensive guys who knew this. I eventually went with Joe Hirshberg who had been a federal prosecutor who specialized in white collar work and he set me back $50,000 to start – I mean to start!

Unfortunately, I was stuck defending the case in the Philadelphia County court system where most of the judges were also unfamiliar with commercial transactions. The local Philadelphia judges are elected by the general public, which means they are all political animals who pay in $450,000 to the political powers. Since the public has no idea who is qualified, we get the bottom of the barrel judges. If I had been in federal court, the judges there are appointed by the President and must pass the scrutiny of the Senate. These jobs are much more prestigious and their cases are much more complex. So I had to hire a thoroughbred to run a plow horse event.

In any case, we showed up for the preliminary hearing at 21st and Winter Street. Since we were near Center City, we drew a big crowd of press and curiosity seekers. The courtroom actually looked like a large public toilet. The walls were covered in blue-green ceramic brick, the ceiling was an industrial drop ceiling and the floor was part ceramic tile, part faded linoleum. I apparently was newsworthy. In a preliminary hearing, I would get to hear more about the case and how they would prove it. But there was a limit. They only had to present a prima facie case – just enough evidence to prove that I had probably committed a crime. I did not get to go into other evidence that might prove I was not guilty. So I was limited at this point to just the bare bones of a case.

My lawyer, however, could press for other information and maybe the judge might allow an inquiry but did not have to. However, since the press was there and since we had a decent crowd, he felt he had to ask questions which raised the possibility of other evidence which might cast doubt on my guilt. After all, this case might be tried in the newspapers and the reporters always enjoyed a good story.

When the case was called, the first witness was from the brokerage firm of Levin and Sharpe and he identified a letter which bore the signature of a partner in our firm. It read:

Re: Millersville Sewer Project Municipal Bond

Dear Mr. Stevenson,
Please wire the proceeds from the bond purchase from Levin and Sharpe to the account of the escrow account of Dimstom, Charter & Fisk. The wire instructions are to Franklin Bank ABA etc.

Very truly yours,
Ivan Gardner

We were shown the document encased in a plastic binder. The witness from Levin and Sharpe explained that they received checks or wires from various brokerage houses whose customers had subscribed to the offering and as the money was received it was forwarded into an escrow account of our law firm handling the closing to be disbursed upon the completion of the closing. She indicated that this letter was handed to her by one of the men handling the sale of the bonds and she complied with the request. My lawyer started his cross:

"Good morning, Ms. Hackett."

"Good morning."

"Which man handed you this letter?"

"I'm not sure. It could have been Mr. Peterson, he usually handled this."

"Did you notice that Mr. Gardner was not involved in the bond closing?"

"Oh, I wouldn't know that."

"Did you notice that this was a different bank account from the one the other checks or wires went into?"

"Oh, I didn't pay attention to that. I just walked the letter over to the wire department, filled out the form and put the copy of the wire receipt in the file."

"Do you know Mr. Gardner?"

"No."

"Do you know if Mr. Peterson knows Mr. Gardner?"

"I don't know. I don't think so?"

"How did the letter come in?"

"By regular mail."

"Did you handle it?"

"Of course, I opened it and took it to one of the men handling the transaction."

"Did they handle it?"

"I believe they did?"

"Do you know who did?"

"No. As I said, I guessed it was Mr. Peterson. I don't remember."

"When did the letter come into your office?"

"April 17 – I can tell by the timestamp. I timestamped all the mail. So I timestamped this on that date."

"Your Honor, no further questions at this time. I would like to hold the witness subject to recall."

"Very well, counsel." The judge turned to the prosecutor.

"Next witness."

"The prosecutor swore in an expert witness in handwriting – a Mr. McKinsey.

"Your Honor, in the interest of time, I see that Mr. McKinsey has a lengthy résumé he is about to testify from. If I could review it just for a bit, I might stipulate for the purpose of the hearing today to his qualifications." My lawyer and I knew we would to an extensive vetting of this witness before trial, so there was no need now to cross-examine him as to his qualifications now.

It seemed Mr. MacKinsey was an expert in handwriting often used by the prosecution cases, but also used on many situations including bad checks, will contests, etc. He was used by the FBI in a number of local matters. We agreed for the time being that he was qualified. So, the prosecutor started.

"Mr. MacKinsey, have you examined this document (referring to the letter)?"

"Yes, I have"

"Whose signature is at the bottom of the letter?"

"I don't know."

"Is it Mr. Gardner's?"

"In my opinion, it is not his signature."

"First, I have examined many of Mr. Gardner's signatures and it does not match any of them."

"Can you explain?"

With that, Mr. MacKinsey flashed on the screen six different signatures of Mr. Gardner alongside that of the writing on the letter. He went into detail explaining how the shape of the letters and the spacing of the letters were different.

"So, at this time, you believe that this signature was a forgery."

"I do."

"No further questions."

"Mr. MacKinsey," my lawyer started, "can you tell whether the signature you see was done by someone left handed or right handed?"

"No."

"Are there ink smears by a left handed person or any palm marks by a right handed person?"

"Not that I could tell."

"Was the signature traced from a true signature or was it made free hand?"

"I would side with a free hand drawing, but not for sure. The spacing of the names and the shape of the letters is sufficiently different that I would have to say it was not a tracing, or at best, a very bad tracing effort."

"Can you tell me who might have done this? Was he a male, a female, left handed or right handed, old or young?"

"No, not really. There is a slight left hand slant – which means nothing. The pressure seems to be even and regular."

"In any case, this signature could have been done by anyone?"

"Yes, but it does not appear to be Mr. Gardner's."

"But he could have done it."

"Yes, I suppose so."

"Okay, no further questions."

The assistant district attorney "ADA" next called Ivan Gardener.

"Mr. Gardner, you are a member of the firm of Dunstan, Charter & Fisk."

"Yes."

"Have you seen this letter?"

"Just recently."

"Did you sign that signature at the end?"

"No, I did not," he said between clenched teeth, unwavering in his angry stare at me.

"Did you send the letter?"

"No, I did not."

"Your witness, Mr. Hirshberg."

"Mr. Gardner, did you have access to the firm stationary?"

"Of course."

"Had you participated in municipal bond financings in the past?"

"Yes, but only peripherally. Only when some real estate expertise was required. The bond department handled everything usually."

"Was Mr. Jacobson familiar with bond financings?"

"To some degree, he did bits and pieces of work assigned to him."

"Did he have any contract with the brokerage firms?"

"Not to my knowledge.

"Did you?"

"Not directly, no."

"And you know $3.1 million was coming to your firm from Levin and Sharpe?"

"I can't say that I did."

"Were you aware of the Millersville Bond closing?"

"I can't say that I was."

"Were you aware of the Millersville Bond closing?"

"In general terms, yes. I knew our firm was doing it."

"Did Mr. Jacobson know about $3.1 million coming to your firm?"

"From what I hear, he must have. He stole it, didn't he?"

"Well, isn't that to be determined?"

"Not in my mind."

"Your honor, I ask that these remarks be stricken."

"Yes, Mr. Gardner, you know the law. Answer the question that is asked, don't give us your opinion."

"I don't know what Mr. Jacobson knew or didn't know for a fact. Ask him."

"Objection, your honor."

"Yes, Mr. Gardner. Please you know the defendant has a right not to testify. Fortunately, this is a preliminary hearing and your remarks have no meaning. At the time of trial, I suggest you be more disciplined."

"Yes, your honor."

"Mr. Gardner, have you received any sums from the Cayman Islands lately?" What the hell, it was a flier, but he was being an ass, so could we?

"What...? What does that mean?"

"Please answer the question."

"No. Of course not. Are you accusing me of something?"

"This is just cross examination."

"Who has the initials IRG? As shown at the bottom of this letter."

"I do."

"And who has the initials 'SSM'?"

"I don't know."

"What do the initials mean if they appear on the letter?"

"SSM would mean the initials of the typist."

"Where were you on the date this letter was sent?"

"In the office."

"Where was Mr. Jacobson?"

"I don't know. Probably at the office."

"No further questions at this time."

The ADA next called Grace Hollister.

"Ms. Hollister, where do you work?"

"At Franklin National Bank."

"In what office?"

"The Center City branch."

"What did you do?"

"I was an Assistant Vice President and Relationship Manager, so I had a variety of responsibilities. I opened accounts, answered customers' questions, sent out wires, - in short, almost anything that tellers do, plus a number of other operations."

"I am showing you some documents and ask if you have seen them before."

"Yes, these are documents I handled to open a new account at the bank. It was an escrow account for the law firm of Dimstom, Charter & Fisk. It used its Federal Identification Number, and had signature cards."

"Who opened the account?"

"Joseph Jacobson."

"Do you know today who that is?"

"Yes, the man in the suit sitting over there," pointing at me.

"How do you remember him?"

"He came in a suit and he was from the firm of Dimstom, Charter & Fisk. We always gave good service to people from his firm."

"Why did you allow an associate of the law firm to sign and open this account?"

"I didn't know what he was. He was from our law firm."

"How do you know that?"

"He was on the letterhead."

"But wasn't he near the bottom of the letterhead?"

"Yes, but how was I to know if he was authorized?"

"So, you just let him sign for the entire firm?"

"Yes."

"Now, how about the signature cards? Who signed them?"

"They were delivered later."

"So the men whose signatures appear on the signature cards never appeared?"

"No. The cards were delivered later. I don't know how."

"Didn't this transaction at your desk take place under a camera? Wasn't it recorded on a CD?"

"Yes, probably."

"So, where is the CD?"

"It was probably erased. They recycle every month. So, the old recording is erased."

"Did the police ever ask to see the CD?"

"I don't know."

"So, the only way to prove that Mr. Jacobson was the one who appeared at your desk to open this new escrow account for the law firm is your testimony as to your recollection from three months ago?"

"Yes. I guess so."

"Have you ever been given or promised anything to give testimony against Mr. Jacobson in this matter?"

"I resent that."

"Well, yes or no."

"No. Absolutely no."

"Alright. No further questions."

The ADA then called Horace Heim from Incorporations.com.

"Mr. Heim, do you recognize this document?"

"Yes, it is our online order form for a complete corporation kit."

"So who ordered what on the form?"

"A Mr. Jacobson ordered a corporation agreement, and a registration form for the Commonwealth of Pennsylvania which he had filled out."

"So you did what with this form?"

"We filed it with Pennsylvania and sent him a copy of confirmation and a receipt copy from Pennsylvania."

"Who paid for this transaction?"

"I see that Mr. Jacobson paid for this online with his credit card."

"Does the information on his order conform to the copy of the credit card I have marked as Exhibit 4."

"Yes, those were all the correct numbers for the charges."

"No further questions."

My lawyer then asked, "Could someone who had access to Mr. Jacobson's credit card information have made this order?"

"Yes. It was all done online. So as long as the credit card was approved, we completed the order. We never saw who did it."

That was about all for the witnesses. My lawyer got up and made a nice argument that all the evidence was circumstantial – no one had actually said I took the money. The judge at this level had to say however, that there was enough evidence to possibly find me guilty in the future. He was right as far as that went. I would have to have a conference with my lawyer to review everything and decide what would happen next.

Oh, I should mention that Bonnie gave me a call after the six o'clock news – could we meet? What was this – a pep talk, a commiseration, a breakup – what?

It seemed to me that men and women are different. No shit. I can't be the first person to discover this. But Bonnie, and I think most women, are social creatures and see their men as social animals in a social context. Perhaps women have an innate or deeply acculturated need for safety and protection. They look to men with power, or prestige in the community. In high school, it is the star football player; when his image fades, they seek professional men, men of political standing. Men on the other hand like to idealize their women, make them into an exotic icon, on a pedestal. Some with purity and innocence, some with sensuality and beauty. But they see their women as their own – they will defend her image to the world and her reputation with it. I couldn't blame Bonnie, nor even call her shallow or stupid. She thought she had a high ranking lawyer, a pillar of the community, a good provider. She had not bargained for the romantic role of long suffering convict's wife. She needed a new provider and fast.

On the other hand, when I say on the other hand, it is my legal training that forces this on me. It is always necessary to understand the opposing or competing view. Much of Western culture is based on two images of two Marys. So men have been given the choice of Madonna or Virgin. Why can't we chose from Esther, Rachel, Deborah, Tamar? Was I looking for the Virgin Mary? Then again, what do I now? One more thing to ponder in my enforced house of solitude. Was I supposed to be learning something?

I don't need to say that at our meeting Bonnie broke it off. She was angry and hurt that "I could do such a thing." She didn't believe me. What was I supposed to learn from this?

After the preliminary hearing, I sat with Hirshberg to review. But thinking back, I would have to say maybe early April, it would have been known around the office that there was a Millersville bond financing. By the way, this may or may not help. That letterhead on which the letter was written was not the current letterhead at the time. I will find out when the letterhead was replaced. It may have been late March, and the letter is dated April 17. See, we change letterhead every six months, because our partners change and our associates come and go. So we update to the current lineup every six months. Also, as you can see, I was not on the partner side of the letterhead, I was near the bottom of the associate's page and Gardner was near the top of the associates. You see all partners are ranked in terms of seniority in the firm, and they appear listed in order on the right. Similarly, associates are listed in order on the right."

"So anyone looking at the letterhead would know if you were a partner or an associate by looking at the current letterhead?" Hirshberg asked.

"Yes."

"So this lady from the bank would know you were not a partner."

"Since she handled many things for our firm, I would have to say yes."

"So she would know you were not a partner and not authorized to open an account in the firm's name."

"Yes."

"Now she is the key to the case."

"Had you ever seen her before?"

"Yes. Everyone in the firm may have done banking business through her. She is our "Relationship Manager.""

"So she had access to all your bank information, your accounts, etc."

"Yes."

"How about your debit card?"

"I don't know how far she can get into that. Maybe, maybe not."

"She wouldn't know my pin, but she might know the numbers appearing on the card. She could charge things over the phone."

"Would anyone else know the numbers, etc. on your card?"

"Probably yes. It was used by secretaries to order lunch sometimes. It appeared on my receipts to claim my expense money. I gave it to Gardner sometimes if we had to go to a lunch or dinner meeting to split the bill. I could probably think of more times."

"Well, basically, as I see it: Anyone could have had a stash of the old stationery and forged the letter directing the $3.1 million wire. A number of people could have used your debit card. Gardner among them. The lady at the bank has to be lying about you and must be in on the setup. It is more than coincidence that no one kept the CD from the camera filming the transaction. That would exonerate you. It might even nail someone else.

"So, I think the lady at the bank and two or more people from your firm set this up. They had to devise the plan while the old stationery was available, saved the stationery, got it typed up and forged Gardner's signature. Someone had to be familiar with the municipal bond financing process and had to know early on about the Millersville bond financing. So that's what we have to work on.

"I will get out some subpoenas and file some discovery motions to get at whatever there is that may help us. Meanwhile, do some of your own thinking."

As if I was not thinking every waking minute. What was I doing April 17, who had used my debit card, what would the bank now, what would the people in the law firm know and when. It went on over and over in my head, even at 2:00 a.m. or 5:00 p.m. or whenever I had nothing else to do but think about this arrest.

I knew at least that we needed a full background check on the lady at the bank, I would like to see her bank account activity and that of Ivan Gardner. We should get all the bank documents on this series of transactions.

BACK IN PRISON

My reverie over the preliminary hearing kept floating in and out as I lay on my back in my prison bed. I had barely existed as waves of depression swept over me. Where had it all gone wrong? The evidence was fairly weak, and I had hopes for the trial. I shivered as I remembered the lead up to the trial. Then, Satchel came in.

"Look, Jake (my new name in the joint) I'm tired of you moping around. It's our turn on the weights in the yard. Now, get off your ass and come down."

The weights were a very guarded area in the yard. The different groups had priority in terms of their power in the prison population. The Muslims got first priority, then the drug lords, then the gangs – black teenage, motor cycle/meth gangs – eventually the older black guys. Because I ate with Satchel and his buddies, I was counted among them, so I was included with them in our dining hall status and now our turn on the weights. I had become an "Older Black Guy."

I tagged along behind Satchel to the yard where the rest of the older black guys were stretching and warming up. We started on the bench first. We all did a warmup set at 135 and kept going up at 10 pound intervals with different guys dropping out if they couldn't get at least three reps. I waited as the bar went up to 225, I knew I could warm up with six reps there. By now, our group was down to six. Everyone was standing around talking trash, laughing and panting as guys dropped out. Of course, I was at least 10 years younger than anyone, and at 175 pounds I was one of the smaller guys. At 265, there were three of us left. I did four reps to stay in. But by now, I was attracting a crowd. The other groups lounging around the yard, smoking, jiving, talking would see the new guy – a smallish white dude was doing decent weight on the bench bar. I got three reps at 275 along with the other two dudes – one weighting in at least 250 and the other – an immense guy at 300 pounds at least. I missed my third rep at 285 and sat down – to much applause and back slapping from the older black dudes – I was a bit of a celebrity now and I was their celebrity among the other groups. My mood brightened, my endorphins were flowing, and I grinned modestly. It was my regular trips to an expensive gym that was saving me – a decent investment. Satchel took personal pride in my debut and refused to leave my side as we went through the rest of the weights – dumbbells on the incline bench, lat pulldowns, leg presses, delt raises, tri skull crushes, and lastly chins. Because of my weight, I also won the chins doing 15 solid ones. The older black guys claimed me, slapped me on the back and looked around to see if the other groups noticed. I guess they did.

We trooped into lunch, with the older guys trash talking the white gangs, especially the motorcycle/meth guys. They missed out on this white draft pick. I was too clean to be a gang banger anyway. Lunch was a fun time now. The other guys come by and slapped five. Satchel's group had moved out of the cellar. They had always ranked above the solitary weirdos, the child molesters, the clueless wife killers, and the really old guys. We were now, at least, a thing. We tumbled into the mess hall, I on a wave of euphoria.

Looking back, Satchel had done me a service. I immediately returned the favor by writing two of my friends each of whom owned a restaurant. Satchel needed someone to agree to employ him if he was to be transferred to a halfway house. I asked each of my friends if they could find a place for him. I vouched for his character and good nature. One felt he was too upscale to have an ex con, but the other not only was happy to respond but had found a program where he would be compensated for half of the wages he paid. He wrote an enthusiastic letter agreeing to employ Satchel and addressed it to the Warden.

As I began to be recognized around the yard, it became known that I had been a lawyer. Of course, I did not practice criminal law but at least knew how to do research. Since Satchel was recognized as my protector, different people would sidle up to him and ask if I would agree to at least hear their story. Satchel was now a man of power, my gatekeeper.

"Let me see if I can help you. I haven't been disbarred yet. What do you want? Halfway house, parole," I asked Satchel.

"I have two sisters left in Philadelphia, so I think a halfway house there."

"I could get you a job, I think. What can you do?"

"Oh, I was a bartender. I had been at the Ritz Carlton for five years. You should see me in one of those spiffy uniforms. I can also cook."

"Okay, a halfway house and a bartending job. Let's work on that."

By this time, we got to the dining hall and I sat with Satchel and his buddies. The dinner wasn't too bad – mystery meat in gravy, mashed potatoes and some overcooked string beans. Satchel and his buddies were all older cons, in their 50s and 60s, ignored by the rest of the population. They talked about old times, and the Eagles. Satchel, of course, bragged that his cellie was a lawyer.

After Lift and Lunch

After lunch, I retired to my bunk for a nap, but my mind would not shut down. With the euphoria and endorphinic rush of the workout, my despair had turned to anger. Anger at the turn of events prior to and during my trial.

My lawyer and I compiled a list of areas to be investigated, researched and nitpicked. First was a complete background review of Ms. Hollister – the bank employee who had identified me as opening the phony bank account. Her prior life was unremarkable. She came from a nice blue collar family and had attended a local parochial school, had taken the business course rather than the academic course which lead to college. Her father had a DUI and was a heavy drinker. The family had good credit. Her mother worked as a sales clerk in a chain store. Her father was a long time railroad employee. Her four brothers and sisters were unremarkable. Her salary at the bank was not large and she was up for review.

She had obviously made a large mistake – completely contrary to the training manual. Opening bank accounts are subject to scrutiny by not only the bank, but by bank examiners from the state and federal departments. They "protect" the dollar and insure that banks follow the rules. To open a bank account without proper ID was a violation of everyone's rules. If a corporation, the officers had to show that the corporation was legitimate by coming in with their Articles of Incorporation, and a copy of the minutes of the corporation showing the officers were authorized to open an account. In this way the federal and state governments could trace the funds through known channels attributable to specific individuals. Partnerships had similar rules. Allowing someone whom she knew or should have known was not a partner in the firm to open an account and then wire funds to a bank in the Cayman Islands was a major breach of the rules of the bank. Her excuse that she handled many transactions for the law firm, and did not feel she should insist on a strict enforcement of the rules was absurd to anyone who was a lawyer or familiar with bank procedure. She should not receive a very good review.

In the overall picture, the bank was insured and so within a short period of time was reimbursed for the $3.1 million dollars that had disappeared and it had to pay out to the law firm. Actually, since the bank was liable along with the law firm, their insurance carriers split the loss between them. All the bank and the law firm suffered was a small financial black eye.

Almost every other transaction could have been executed by anyone in the law firm. The letter, the filing of corporate papers, charging the fee to my debit card at the bank; anyone could have been done by someone else. There was no direct proof of my exclusive involvement except the testimony of Ms. Hollister.

I had an uneasy feeling about the relationship between the bank and the law firm. The law firm was not only the lawyer for the bank, but had placed several of its associates who had not made partner as house counsel for the bank. The law firm sent lots of business the bank's way – all manners of business, estates, will clients, and everything from smaller, less influential lawyers. The bank's main office was on the street floor and several other floors of the building in which our firm leased its three floors. The bank was simply an elevator ride away and virtually every department in the law firm had some use for the bank. Ms. Hollister handled a large volume of the firm's business. So this relatively minor flub of the $3.1 million theft was certainly not going to interfere with the relationship between the bank and the firm.

My attorney submitted dozens of requests for information to pry out any unusual transaction by any of the firm's lawyers, such as unusual income, which were soundly resisted by the district attorney, the bank and the law firm. We were stonewalled.

And then another piece of bad news. Judge Rosenwald who had originally been assigned the case was removed from the case and Judge Hawley was put on it. We had felt comfortable with Judge Rosenwald. He had some experience as a business lawyer, was Jewish and had represented unions – he came from a humble background and could be considered a liberal. We felt he would be sympathetic to me.

Judge Hawley was a conservative and a member of the local prestigious Republican club where because he was a republican judge his membership was free. He regularly ate at a "club table" where members without a lunch reservation could always walk in and sit. Republican lawyers frequently sat at the table and could be heard discussing "hypothetical" cases with the judge, who often could be found to sit on their cases. He was a drunk and not very bright. Most inept judges assigned to criminal cases relied on the prosecuting ADAs in cases who usually were well prepared and could bully the judge into ruling their way. It was also the safest path for a judge. If the ADA lost, the criminal defendant simply walked and the ADA had no appeal rights. If he won, the defendant had years of appeal and could straighten things out later.

Unfortunately, we had already agreed to waive a jury trial and be tried by the knowledgeable Judge Rosenwald. When the powers that be switched the calendar listing to Judge Hawley, I had an ominous sense that we were being screwed over.

And that we were. We got adverse ruling after adverse ruling. Veteran lawyers were starting to comment off the record to the press. No one had the stones to comment on the record against a sitting judge. My lawyer kept making his trial notes and muttering "error bag." An error bag is what a trial lawyer puts all the appealable issues into for his appellate brief. Unfortunately, it takes years to get these before an appellate court and is one more chance for an unpredictable result.

Although we were able to demonstrate that many different members of the firm could have set up this transfer and claimed the money, Ms. Hollister was able to testify that I alone set up the account. We made many attempts to discredit this testimony. First, it was just too obvious. Why would a reasonably intelligent lawyer set up an account right under the firm's nose in a bank that would easily be able to pick out the one who opened the account? Anyone would know to open the account in an obscure bank where he might not be recognized. The disappearance of the CD from the bank's camera which might back up Hollister's testimony was an unbelievable coincidence. But to come to these conclusions, the judge would have to find something was perhaps bad at the law firm. While the judge did not have to find me innocent, he only had to suspect that there was reasonable doubt as to whether I was guilty. This was too much for the judge. He caved into the prosecutor, and found me guilty.

But the "error bag" was full. In a time without a jury, just in front of a judge, the errors which gave you a new trial were very limited. Where the judge was the trier of fact, the range of errors was vastly expanded. We could take another shot at another, and perhaps better judge if the appellate court found judge Hawley was the stupid, biased, drunk that he was. Pure and simple.

Under normal circumstances, I could remain free on bail pending appeal. Now here's the kicker. The judge found that since he believed I had $3.1 million stashed, I could run away and hide, he cancelled my bail and ordered me into jail forthwith. A gaspingly harsh move. I had been screwed. No reason I was depressed. Not only was I innocent, but at every turn I was screwed. I replayed the trial over and over in my head. I felt the depth of despair only Franz Kafka could feel. I even began to search my soul for justification for my state. Had I done something else wrong for which I was being punished? Was I somehow deluded in my mind and was I actually guilty? The entire system had come down on me. I moped through dinner and went to sleep to a kaleidoscope of distorted images from my past. I lay in bed for hours and slept lightly, in nightmare vision for most. Until I could hear Satchel, "Jake, Jake, come on it's breakfast." I got up and went to breakfast. Big Henry had adopted me also – Henry Worthington went about 320 and stood 6 foot 4. His voice rumbled and shook the bars of my cell. Fortunately, Henry had an entrepreneurial mentality. He wanted to rent me out to the other prisoners to see if I could help them. He would serve as my appointments secretary and allow people to run their cases by me to see if there was any hope.

After breakfast, Henry got me a small room in the library that was supposed to be a computer room, but the warden couldn't figure out how to block porn or other banned communications so the room sat empty with a dead donated Dell computer in it. I sat next to the Dell.

The first prisoner came in. I gave him the usual lecture that if he lied, or made up a story, or didn't tell me the whole truth, our talk was useless. Actually, almost all the prisoners were already convicted and were serving their sentence. Their appeal rights were very slim at this point. Some guys were already convicted of one crime and facing conviction on another. Most of the time the guys had had court appointed counsel, and if they could prove the lawyer had been incompetent or "ineffective," they could get a new trial. Most lawyers did not like to handle "ineffective assistance of counsel cases," because they didn't want to rat out their brothers. I was in no frame of mind to protect other lawyers and got a decent therapy by critiquing those sad sack attorneys who relied on court appointments for a living.

Each prisoner had one hour and I reviewed each case carefully and made notes. I handwrote a series of instructions to a prisoner who knew how to type up the ineffective assistance motions with citations to the appropriate laws.

I have to admit I felt energized by the process. It got my mind off me, and gave me a chance to demonstrate the faults with a legal system. Soon, we were churning out two or three motions a day. Most of the time, the convict had told the lawyer about witnesses the lawyer failed to call, or documents the lawyer failed to subpoena. Often they failed to argue cases about search warrants, or illegal arrests, constitutional rights that were violated. At the very least, it gave the men hope. It definitely irritated the trial lawyer and the prosecutor. After a few months, we might begin to win a few. At the very least, the men were sent notices that there would be a hearing on their motion. Not a win, not even a new trial, but a day or two away from the grinding monotony of prison life and a chance at a new trial.

Henry meanwhile as gatekeeper was collecting prodigious amounts of cigarettes, marijuana, pills, toiletries – the currency of prison life. I now had a stack of 10 tubes of toothpaste, and 12 bars of soap. The get-togethers of the old black men's group were beclouded with enough marijuana smoke to zone out an entire city block. The guards always looked the other way because a zoned-out prisoner was a happy prisoner and less likely to cause trouble. The guards who actually trafficked in pot were not unhappy because, of course, it was their pot that was being traded and smoked. And the old black guys group including this one young white Jewish guy steadily rose in status and influence. My mood rose. I was accorded respect in the halls of the lock up.

I had now begun to develop a structure to my life in the hoosegow. I had breakfast with kindred souls, either went to the yard to lift weights or held court listening to stories of the prisoners. In a way my discipline in the law, the bout of legal thinking became a form of ritual, not unlike prayer. A familiar series of exercises, a repetition of beliefs. My ritual was preserving my sanity. I was becoming human again. The mental and physical balance of exercise began to let me sleep. My dreams were no longer exaggerated reenactments of the arrest and trial, the repeated investigation into the unyielding chain of events to seek out my enemies. They now included the hopes and dreams of the prisoners whose stories I had heard. I was drawn outside myself and invited to unlock legal puzzles in an abstract objective manner- from a distance. This combined with the weightlifting in the yard acted to strengthen me.

SATCHEL'S HEARING

Satchel appeared for his parole hearing. As a still disbarred lawyer, I was permitted to attend and speak on his behalf. I was astounded though at the parole board. When I reviewed their respective resumes, they were all political appointees with little or no experience in criminal law, psychology, sociology, even religion. They were mostly hacks looking for a few pay days to shore up their meager earnings. There were a few comments on Satchel's behavior, his work record, his peers or his guards. It was worse than sentencing where a judge also with no training, evaluates the sum total of another human's life and assigns him to a mind numbing nothingness for a period of time. I saw this as a gap I had to fill as an advocate. Rarely do these largely inarticulate, poorly educated prisoners have anyone to define their character and eligibility for freedom.

Satchel appeared as his usual pleasant, eager to please passive self and recited the usual lines convicts are schooled to recite about remorse, and asking for a second chance. The board was bored, as expected.

I was able to recite some quotes from his fellow inmates about his kindness, from his guards about his leadership, from his prison work job about his uncomplaining willingness to do the job at hand in the kitchen, and his personal dedication seeing the food was well prepared, that he was a dedicated cook.

I described how he personally drew me back from the edge of despair. And I finished with the letter from my friend who owned a restaurant, offering him a job if he was placed in a halfway house.

This chance to be a lawyer again drew me out of my funk. Satchel was so grateful. No one had ever gone to bat for him like this before.

Big Henry and Squiffy

Along with Satchel, Big Henry had allowed his not inconsiderable girth to edge his way in as my protector and social secretary. Of course, Big Henry was never far from Squiffy – born Alfred Chatsworth of Columbia Avenue, North Philadelphia, Pennsylvania. Both he and Henry were more street smart than Satchel. Satchel had been misled into being a getaway driver for a heist, but Henry and Squiffy were minor league drug dealers. Both affable, friendly with good sales personalities. With a decent education they could have been factory reps, stock brokers, but by eleventh grade their hormones took over and the images on the TV of fast cars, fast women, casinos got the better of the image from high school of a sober responsible citizen with verbal and math skills. A familiar refrain. They were knocking down $1,000 a week by the time they were 18, tax free of course. Better than to be an apprentice somewhere at $10 per hour. Squiffy went about 5'6" and 130 pounds, but could run. Big Henry was over twice his size, but they were cellies and now the leaders of the old black guy group in the joint – a position they wore with considerable pride although we were at the bottom of the heap otherwise.

As I sat in my designated office the defunct, but funded computer room doing some legal research, Squiffy knocked on the door.

"Squiff-mesiter. What can I do for you?"

"I got this dude, and he looks scary. He got biker tats and a mean streak."

"Show my first customer of the day in, but hang by the door with some backup."

"Gotcha."

In walked, as advertised a mean hunk of a dude – 6'3" about 240 and cut. I mean his muscles had muscles. He had two gold stars on his front teeth and a head scarf on his shaved head. He had the fashion choice of the prison population – an orange jumpsuit. When he took to the weights in the yard, he sported a shredded wife beater (a white tank top). Around the prison, we all wore the generic jump suit.

"What can I do for you?"

"I don't know, man. I need advice."

"Okay, what's your story?"

"I'm a member of the Devil's Spawn and we work out of Chester County."

"What's your name, first?" I was taking notes – still confidential since I had not yet been disbarred.

"Vincent. Vincent Spadafora. But they call me Jax or Ajax."

"Okay, Jax. What can I do for you?"

"I'm serving two to four on a minor drug beef. I got caught carrying a ki of meth."

"Was that a righteous bust?"

"Yeah. I was a bit high and got into a road rage thing with a guy on Route 1, and the cops broke it up. But my tailgate was open, 'cause I was gonna get my tire iron. They could see the meth in the back."

"Uh-oh. Not good."

"Yeah, the lawyer told me to plead, so I did and made up a story about my supplier so I got leniency."

"Okay, so far so good."

"Well, not so good. Me and two other dudes took down a biker bar in Chester and beat up a few guys in the smack down. We got away and made a nice haul of their stash. The cops in Chester couldn't figure it out, so I figured we were in the clear. Then, this task force guy started doin' DNA, and fiber shit on the scene all over again. The lawyer says to lay low. But two of the guys we hit just died. I mean dead. I've never done that before. The autopsy is bad. I mean bad... bad shit."

"How have you seen the autopsy?"

"One of the guys got arrested for it from his prints and the lawyer gave it to him."

"Who is this lawyer?"

"Joe Devlin. He does all our work."

"You mean he represents everyone from your gang that gets arrested?"

"Yep."

"So have you been named yet?"

"No. But the other guy… the one who got arrested, may be talking. We don't know."

"I don't, but Devlin came in to see me, and he was cute. He wouldn't say nothing, but he was asking me where I stood. I told him, I didn't do it, but I could tell he didn't believe me."

"Okay, Jax or shall I call you Vincent?"

"Jax, that's who I am now."

"Okay, Jax, this Devlin has what we call a conflict of interest. His loyalty is to the gang since they pay him, not you."

"Okay."

"And who knows what this other guy is saying, especially about you. You know he who rats first, rats best. So how can they make you?"

"I don't know."

"Was there a surveillance camera at the bar?"

"Maybe, I don't know."

"Was there a surveillance camera on the block?"

"Yeah, I think so."

"Were you riding your bikes or did you have a car?"

"We had a van."

"With a valid license plate."

"Yeah, but it was stolen."

"Where is the van now?"

"The cops took it."

"Who was the driver?"

"Me."

"Were you wearing gloves?"

"Yeah before. I think I took them off to whale on this one dude."

"Did you drive away without the gloves on?"

"I don't' remember."

"What did you beat these guys with?"

"Chains, bicycle chains."

"Did they have oil on them?"

"For sure."

"Were you wearing gloves when you were 'whaling'?"

"Probably."

"Where are the chains now?"

"They were in the van."

"Did these guys hit you?"

"They got a few licks in."

"Did you bleed?"

"Maybe, my lip and my forehead."

"Do you think you dripped blood at the scene?"

"Can't tell."

"Did you get stitches?"

"No, just butterflies. One of the bitches keeps butterflies."

"So, it was definitely an open bleeding wound."

"For sure."

"Were there any witnesses?"

"Maybe the bar maid."

"Where was she?"

"She ran out with everyone else when I swung the chains on the bar."

"So everyone else saw you."

"Could be."

"They may rat you out."

"No one rats us out in Chester County. Believe me, no one rats us out."

"But she could be upset about losing her boyfriend."

"Nah. She gets passed around."

"Do you know her?"

"I seen her sometimes in high school. But she's a skank. She gets passed around."

"Okay, anything else?"

"I can't think of anything."

"How did they get this guy who was in on it with you?"

"He got picked up on a federal bust, a sale a few weeks ago."

"When did he get picked up?"

"Two days after our takedown of the bar."

"Describe the other guys with you in this raid."

"Well, Cap is about 5'10" with a gray beard and he's the VP of the club, takes in the dues, and Big Joey is about 5'10" my age, but skinny."

"So you are the only big guy."

"Yeah."

"So who did most of the beating?"

"Me."

"Did they carry weapons?"

"Both had guns."

"What did you have?"

"Just the chains."

"Well, Jax. I hate to say this but I've got bad news for you. First, I think you're gonna go down for the killing in the bar, and I think you could be looking at Murder 1 with the death penalty. I think from the evidence you guys left behind, the feds will make you. The feds are not like the Chester cops, they don't scare easily and they do get people to talk because federal sentences are long and you only get a lighter sentence if you spill your guts.

"First, the bar maid may talk. Then, your prints may be on the chain or the van, your blood may be in the bar or on the van, the cameras may have caught you. And you, you stand out, Jax. Both of the other guys were smaller, you are big and in your tank top, you are shall I say conspicuous.

"Plus, they got Cap on two charges. He could be looking at over 25 years to life. He may make a deal and rat you out. Even if they also only have enough evidence to convict you, he will get a nice benefit by ratting you out."

"So, what do I do?"

"What did Devlin tell you to do?"

"Lay low and keep quiet."

"My take on this is they may be setting you up. This lawyer Devlin owes his loyalty to the Devil's Span, not to you, because that's who pays him. A lawyer is supposed to be loyal to his client – meaning you. Cap is higher in rank than you in the club. Right?"

"Yeah. He's been there for years. I've just been in two years."

"So, Devlin is more loyal to him than he is to you. Now, how about this Joey."

"Joey's been in for years. He's best buds with Cap."

"So it was their takedown of this bar, and they brought you along for the muscle."

"I guess so."

"So maybe Cap will rat you out to save his ass, and leave out Joey. Then you get Murder 1 and Cap gets off lighter. You could be looking at the death penalty."

"Whoa!"

"Now, look you don't pay me. You want honest advice, that's what I give. I don't have a loyalty to anyone but you and I don't need to soft pedal this because I want to get paid."

"Well, we gave you a couple ounces of weed."

"True enough, but some lawyers say they will get you off or get a light sentence as you will keep making payments. I don't need that. I personally think there is too much evidence out there that can point to you, and I am suspicious that Cap may rat you out on Devlin's advice."

"What do I do?"

"You have two choices. One – call the cops now, tell them the whole story off the record but through your lawyer – called a "proffer deal" and make a deal for a lighter sentence. Give all the details about Cap and Joey and tell them how much remorse you have about what happened. Lay the chains on Cap or Joey. Grow your hair out, clean yourself up, and plead to third degree felony murder and get 5 to 10 years on a state sentence.

"Second, wait until they arrest you and review all the evidence. See if there are any holes in it and hope that good things happen at trial like government or prosecutor screw-ups. Then, if that doesn't happen, hope you don't get the death penalty. If you get life, you may in 15 or 20 years get a parole if you have been extra, extra good, but very unlikely."

"I can't rat out Cap and Joey."

"Joey is your key to a deal, because they may not know about Joey yet."

"No. Can't do that. First they'd kill me. But I can't do it anyway."

"They won't kill you. I can get you segregated. That means put in a prison far away from the Devil's Spawn."

No. Can't do it. Won't do it."

"Okay. That's my advice."

"That's the best you can do."

"'fraid so."

As I said this, I could see a tremor shake through Jax' body – a visible tremor. This huge hulk of a man began to shiver and tear up. I looked around to make sure no one else could see – an admission of weakness in prison was a harbinger of death. "I'm sorry, Jax, what can I do?"

"Sorry, sir." (Sir? Was I now a sir) "I'm afraid."

"Can't do anything?"

"I need to call my mother." Jax was a good Italian son and obviously had a strong attachment to his mother. "She warned me about this."

"'Jax… I started.

"Call me Vincent. That's who I really am. I should have stayed in culinary school, but I had to be tough. The world expected it of me."

"Ah, so you're a cook."

"Actually, I'm a very good cook. But I learned to cook meth. Well, not do the cooking, more the baking. I helped dry out the crystals when we got into the cooking end of the business."

"What can you cook otherwise?"

"Actually, I bake – cakes, tortes, cannolis, tiramisu, macaroons, you name it. Any French pastry."

"Why did you switch to the biker gang?"

"I was a big guy and someone always wanted to fight me to prove themselves. Little guys wanted me around. I just got to be that way."

"No drugs, no sex, drugs and rock and roll."

"Well, some of that, but mainly I just was in the tough gang in my high school, so I went into the tough gang afterwards."

"But your baking skills?"

"I coulda had a scholarship to culinary school, but I was making too much money. I bought my mom a house."

"What are you gonna do now?"

"I can't rat out the gang, and I can't beat the rap it seems."

"Well, think about it and we'll talk."

"Okay. Thanks for listening."

I too felt tremors as he left. Jax or Vincent had some decent sense in him, how it got lost I don't know. I had a bad feeling for him.

DREAMS

I confided in Satchel, Big Henry and Squiffy my concern for Jax. "Yo, why you upset about this skin head?"

It's just that I'm a lawyer. He had become somehow my sacred responsibility.

My mind was comfortably drifting away from my miserable lot, and attaching onto my clients. I began to include them in my fitful dreams. While reliving my own arrest and tried in exaggerated surreal detail, I could also see my new prison clients.

In one, I could see Satchel whistling as he cleaned glasses behind a bar, and handing platters over the bar to customers. He was his usual affable self chatting with patrons, many of whom he knew by name. He had begun to attract an older dinner crowd to the Tavern – older single men mostly, as well as older couples. They talked jazz, and the Philadelphia Warriors, Richie Allen. It was mostly a black crowd in one of the neighborhoods which had started to turn into an upwardly mobile black neighborhood called Mt. Airy. He looked happy.

In another, I could see Jax broken. His head and arms were at odd angles, and he was pale green. His eyes looked up at me imploring, but he didn't move.

These dreams persisted for almost a week. I somehow felt good about the outcome for Satchel.

One morning I could hear hoots and cheers as the halls of the prison rung with shouts. Big Henry was carrying Satchel like a baby and was followed by most of the old black guys contingent. Satchel had a letter in

54

his hand which he was waving and kissing. As they got to our cell, Satchel kept saying, "Thank you, thank you."

"What did I do?"

"I'm going to a halfway house in Nicetown, and I have a job at the Champagne Inn in Germantown."

"Whoa. No shit. What does the letter say?"

"It says I am conditionally transferred to the Nicetown Halfway House at 29th and Allegheny. It has a whole list of conditions but I am released to work at the Champagne Inn from 11:00 a.m. to 7:00 p.m. and I have a leeway of a half hour for transportation. I am not allowed to serve alcohol, but I have to be a cook.Half of my salary goes to the halfway house for room and board. Thank you, thank you."

"That's great, Satchel. Couldn't happen to a nicer guy," and I meant it.

LEON AND REGINALD
IN THE YARD

I was enjoying hanging out with the old black guys in the yeard. Satchel had not left yet for the halfway house – something about waiting for a bed to open up. The usual trash talk, and laments about the Sixers peppered the conversation. After working out on the weights, it was our turn to play in the half court basketball game. I was not a factor in the basketball game – I had a terrible jump shot, so I usually sat and joined in the gibes that belittled the other team. Suddenly, I could feel my mates pull away from me on either side and two new men sat down on either side of me on the bench. I recognized them from around the prison as Tariq al Shabazz and Reginald Blue – they were leaders of the elite black Muslim section. Tariq was known as a major drug kingpin who controlled a large territory in West Philly, and Reginald was known as a superior con-man, an expert in large ventures.

The two men were about the same height about 6'1". Tariq was well built and muscular even in the orange prison jump suit. He wore a knitted Muslim cap. He was quite dark which made his teeth and eyes stood out as almost dazzling white. He had an intense scowl on his face.

Reginald although the same height was rounder and softer looking – not necessarily ____athletic but less imposing. He had a pleasant smile on his light-skinned complexion. Even in prison, he was well groomed – someone had cut his hair neatly and he was quite nice looking.

As they sat down, Reginald said "Yo!" I gave him a "Yo" back. Tariq, on my other side, just nodded. Was I in some kind of trouble? Had I transgressed some unwritten prison rule? Was this a test? Of my manhood? Where was my gang? Especially Big Henry? I looked over at Henry and he just smiled. What did that mean? Was I set up?

Reginald finally broke in. "Can we talk?"

"Sure. What's on your mind?"

"Not here. In the computer room." The computer room was a bit isolated. These two were not known as enforcers. I don't think my physical safety was an issue with them, but who else would I see? I couldn't refuse. Being seen with Tariq and Reginald was somewhat of a social upgrade. Everyone would notice this. We walked up to the computer room and I was about to ask the librarian for a key, when Reginald said, "Never mind, I got one." We all sat around the small table.

I was nervous and managed to get out, "What can I do for you, Mr. Blue?"

"Call me Reggie. We have a few questions and then maybe you can help us."

"Okay, shoot." Somehow I wished I hadn't said exactly that.

"What kind of lawyer are you?"

"Pretty good. I went to a good college and law school and I was with a big firm."

"No. No. We know all that – Yale undergrad, Villanova law review, big firm. Look, we have sources and we've been around."

"I was basically a business lawyer doing mostly real estate."

"So you're not really a criminal lawyer?"

"No, not really."

"You don't hang with the other criminal lawyers?"

"No."

"When we hire criminal lawyers, we get the run of the mill guys who know each other, and have some ins with the judges and the prosecutors. But they talk among themselves."

"I'd have to say that's not me." Was this discussion over?"

"We think that's good. We don't like the choice among those guys. They are a bit too chummy. We want someone independent."

"Well, Reggie. I'm about to be disbarred, I'm sure you know that. So, I can't appear in court, and I can't charge a fee. I come only to give out free advice. That's what I've been doing here."

"So we heard. But Big Henry gets an ounce for your time."

"I'd heard that. Wow! An ounce. That will keep the whole wing high for a few days."

"Do you do weed?"

"Very rarely. I get bad dreams."

"What's that from?"

"You may not believe me, and everyone says it, but I'm innocent and I was set up. Everyone has deserted me and my life got shattered."

"Why do you help these people?"

"Cause I need something to do?"

"At this point, Tariq rumbled in a deep voice. "What if we need some help from you?"

"If I like the problem, I'd be happy to think about it and give you my opinion, Mr. Shabazz."

"Call me Leon."

"Leon?"

"My real name is Leon Jefferson, but that's a slave name. But those who know me still call me Leon." So Reggie and Leon it was.

Reggie began again. "Look, you're smart, real smart and you're independent. We believe we can trust you. If we tell you something, you got to keep your mouth shut."

"I always respect client confidentiality."

"So say all of that rat pack of lawyers we hire, but somehow deals get made. Guys get sold out. Guys rat each other out. We want our own lawyer to give us honest evaluations."

"Fair enough. I can do that. But I'm not a criminal lawyer, and I can't appear in court. I also have to say that criminal law, lots of times, depends on being street smart. I might be a bit too white bread for you."

"Don't worry about that. Leon and I have enough street smarts for all of us. We just want you to consult with us on confidential matters."

"I also have to say, I don't want to be involved in criminal acts. I don't want to help you launder money or plan criminal acts. I wasn't a criminal before, and I don't want to be one now."

"We get that. We won't ask you for that. We want you mostly to listen to what our associates have told us about their cases and tell us what you think. Just like you're doing now. But we want a totally honest answer."

"Honest, I can do."

Tariq/Leon asked first. "I'd like to discuss my situation and see what you make of it."

"Now, Leon, I have to say I won't help you launder money. That's a crime."

"No... No... Nothing like that. Besides, I know all that myself, probably better than you."

"Fine, but I have to speak with you alone. If anyone else hears the conversation, it breaks the attorney-client privilege."

Reggie quickly jumped in. "I know most of it already and I don't need to be there. That's fine. I'll leave now. Let me know when you're done."

As the door closed, Tariq turned to me. "Okay, Mr. Jacobson."

"Call me Jake."

"Okay, Jake. I've gotten into a deal I'm not happy about. Some realtor came to me, and he had the opportunity to buy up a lot of defaulted mortgages and notes. He wanted me to put up the money, Sheriff them out, and buy in houses on the cheap, and resell them."

"Hmm. So far sounds legal, but not very nice."

"That's the point. I may be getting religion but I don't like putting poor folks on the street. And he's been shady with me. So, I want to figure out a way to get him. Legal. No rough stuff."

"Tell me from the beginning how this all arose and let's see what can be done."

"As you know, I have a large number of people working for me in... shall I say – the alternative pharmaceutical industry. Money comes in and I need to find someplace for it. I am bombarded with offers. Some from people you know well and would shock you.

"In any case, a local real estate guy in Germantown came to me and explained that parts of Germantown were getting to be hot areas. The neighboring area, Mt. Airy, was already hot. Partially because the white yuppies were getting along with the buppies – the Black Upwardly Mobile Professionals. Just over Germantown area was a nice stock of houses with good architecture. Some gay guys and some adventurous white pioneers had moved in. So this white realty guy, Labrums wanted to speculate and buy them up while they were cheap. I knew something of this and agreed to go in on it with him.

"But he has a slick way of doing it. He was going to buy all the debts, notes, mortgages from the big banks and credit card companies and foreclose on the properties at below market value even now. So he wanted to move fast and couldn't raise the cash until he sold a few properties, so he asked me to advance the $200,000 he needed to buy up the debts on 40 properties. He showed me charts where he had researched, and he could foreclose on these properties and their present equity value was $600,000 over the first mortgage. If I put up the $200,000 he would pay me back $150,000 in 90 days.

"Although I had only put up 25% then, I would own 50% of the properties. We would sit on them a few years till the neighborhood got hot, and sell them off for $1 million at least. As he explained my investment would be only the $50,000 after he repaid my note. So it seemed like a good idea.

"When he showed me the list of debtors, though, I got some cold feet. I had already paid the $200,000 so I was already in. But either I, my family, or some of my buddies knew the debtors and didn't like the idea of throwing these people out of their houses or stealing their built up equity. I agreed but now I'm stuck. This guy Labrums already has a lawyer working on it. I could be too late. What do I do?"

"Good question. But first, in whose name were these debts acquired, I assume Labrums didn't' want to use your name or his?"

"True. He used the girlfriend of one of my lieutenants as the owner."

"So she is the client. What is her name?"

"Keisha Smallwood."

"How many of your friends, family, etc. know how many of these debtors on the list?"

"I guess of the 40 people, we know at least 30, maybe 35."

"If your friends and family contact them, and give them advice, will they listen?"

"If they say I am behind it, they better goddamn better listen. Especially in Germantown."

"Got it. I mean the advice will be for their own good and may save their homes. We don't need rough stuff only someone they feel they can trust."

"No. I'm sure they'll listen."

"Okay. Let me work on this some and I'll get back to you."

"I'd appreciate it."

JAX

After Leon and I walked out of the computer room and the library, Big Henry and Squiffy were waiting in the hallway. They both couldn't contain themselves.

"What happened? Did he threaten you? Did he want to know about his case?"

"No, guys. I can't say. You know that."

"Are you in danger?"

"No, nothing like that. He wanted legal advice. That's what I gave him. That's all."

"Anything about his case?"

"What case?"

"The one he's got coming up in court?"

"I thought he was already sentenced."

"No. This is a bigger one, a murder."

"No. He didn't discuss it." They seemed disappointed. All these criminal matters were by news at Graterford and Tariq a/k/a Leon was biggest of the news. As he said, he had many associates in the alternative pharmaceutical industry. Big Kenny and Squiffy were minor leaguers, but a shift in the power structure would mean a lot to them.

"We got other news," said Squiffy.

"What's that?"

"You know your man, Jax that you talked to the other day."

"Yeah."

"He got killed."

"By whom, we don't know. He was found in the yard with his neck broke."

"No one knows how?"

"I think lots of people know who and how, but no one's talking."

"But in the yard? Outside? When?"

"They found him in the morning. First shift."

"But the yard is locked all night after dinner and there are guards."

"Ain't it!"

"The guards must have known something or done something!"

"You think."

"Ah. One of those."

"Yeah. One of them."

"I just was speaking to him yesterday."

"Then, you better get your story straight."

"You mean they think I had something to do with it."

"No, but you could be a witness. They gonna talk to you."

"Uh huh. Poor Jax. Underneath he wasn't a bad guy."

"Your day has come!"

Squiffy and Henry just shook their heads. While we were talking, a flunky from Tariq showed up with a brown paper bag and stuck it under Squiffy's arm. Squiffy took a sniff. "Ah… good stuff. Tariq has better connections than us." With that, he slapped me on the back and we walked down to lunch.

CHESTER COPS

It was one of the off days from our time in the yard. I was doing my research for Leon and some of the other guys in the library. The peace and mental stimulation I felt in the library was a blessing. It was comfortable and familiar. I felt some kind of purity. As I pulled out books and scribbled notes, highlighting a few of the better quotes. It was like an intricate treasure hunt, hoping for some glint of hope for one of my guys. About 11:00 a.m., the group of my petitioners would begin to collect outside waiting for me to open my doors to listen to their cases – some hope, no hope, some just wanted to talk and figure out life. I never intended to, but I had been forced into the role of shrink. These men for the most part had no fathers, no guidance, distracted worn-out mothers. They needed a parent. They needed to be told what to do. They had some trust in me, so what I said was meaningful to them even if I was wrong. Some guys were just upset and confused. The best advice I could give was learn how to read and get in some physical fitness routine. This at least gave their life structure.

Anyway, I was listening to my third or fourth guy when two men in sport coats and loosened ties were outside my door and accompanied by prison guards knocked on my inner sanctuary, the computer room.

"Jacobson. Come on out," one of the guards demanded. I came out, looking puzzled. The guards and the two men motioned me out past the line of my customers and over to the Warden's offices. The guards opened the door to a small office and left me with the two men.

"What's this about?" I asked, a bit bewildered.

The two men identified themselves as Chester County detectives. They were both middle aged white guys – even with their sport coats and ties they looked a bit seedy. "When was the last time you spoke to Jax?" Like that, no introductory explanation. Maybe, they thought I was in on his murder.

"Let's see. I have trouble with time in here. I would say Monday, but don't hold me to it. About four days ago."

"Two days before he was murdered?"

"That's right. Yeah. That was two days ago. So it must have been Monday."

"What did you talk about?"

"I can't say. That's attorney – client privilege."

"But he's dead."

"Still holds." Cops hate to hear legal niceties, and especially from lawyers.

"How are you still a lawyer?"

"My case is on appeal. So my conviction isn't final."

"Why aren't you out on bail?"

"The judge thought I might skip bail. What's this about?"

"Jax was a suspect in a bar holdup with the Devil's Spawn gang. We got one of them, but he's not talking. We have some forensics on Jax. We want the third guy."

"Ah. I see. Well. I can't help you."

"You can't or won't."

"Look. I'm in jail because I got framed on an embezzlement charge. I'm not too fond of cops now anyway. Second, I'm in prison with a lot of guys from the Devil's Spawn. If I rat one of them out, I'm a dead man. And, last, why should I help you out, there's no benefit to me and a lot of harm."

"What if we could help you?"

"How?"

"I don't know, ask?"

"I'd like to know how my trial judge got switched from Rosenwald to Hawley? And I'd like a long furlough or even bail."

"We can't do that. We're Chester County, not Philly."

"Okay. I'm Philly not Chester."

"Well, we'll see what we can do."

"Do your best." The men looked at each other, shrugged, and left. Unfortunately, everyone from Chester County in the slammer knew I had been questioned.

Big Henry asked, "What did they want?" He had been waiting in the hall.

"Sorry, Henry. Attorney – client privilege."

By now, it was lunchtime. As usual, we all sat at the old black guys' table, chatting peacefully. Then we could see three of the Devil's Spawn guys walking menacing our way. They stood at our table and the leader, known only as "Dog" said, "I want to speak to the lawyer."

Usually, the white guy gangs and the black guy gangs give each other a wide berth in prison. Probably because they knew a fight was always possible and everyone knew that would lead to no good in prison. The Devil's Spawn guys were breaking an unwritten rule by confronting a black gang, in public for all to see. Granted the old black guys were way down the totem pole, it was a provocation that other black groups might defend. Besides, it was known that I had consulted with Tariq/Leon. So what was so important that the Spawn would challenge us? The dining hall turned to watch.

I asked, "What do you want?"

"Like I said, talk." I knew this was a touchy situation and I did not want to cause trouble for my newly adopted gang.

I turned to the guys at the table. "Look, I'll handle this. Relax." I turned back to Dog and said, "Over there." I pointed to an empty table in the corner.

I wanted to be in clear view of everyone in the dining hall. While we met, I hoped that my burgeoning array of clients at least had my best interests at heart. I had already had dozens of sessions with prisoners who had marital problems, debt problems, small children problems, real estate problems – all for free or at least something small for Big Henry. So I sat with the Spawn.

Dog was a fat guy with a big reddish gray beard and a bald head. His one assistant was a wiry muscular guy with oily black hair and a face full of acne. His other retainer was a large pleasant looking blond guy with a dumb expression on his face.

"What can I do for you?"

"What did you tell the Chester dicks?"

"Nothing. I told them anything I heard was protected by attorney – client privilege. So I sent them on their way."

"Are you sure?"

"Of course, I don't owe them anything."

"What did they ask about?"

"Again, attorney-client privilege. I can't tell you either."

"So it was about something someone said to you."

"Look. I can't even answer that."

"It was Jax, wasn't it?"

"Look, I can't even tell you. I'm still a lawyer, I can't even tell you that."

"We got it. But the cops are looking into a heist that Jax was involved in. We think Jax was gonna cooperate and get a deal. We think you told him to do that. That would put one of ours in on the deal. We want to know about that."

"What did Jax say to you?"

"He wasn't talking, just moping around."

"So why was he killed?"

"He wasn't talking."

"So you figured he was about to rat?"

"Something like that."

"But rat on who?"

"The cops already got Cap for this. We knew Jax was in on it. There was a third. Jax could rat the third guy."

"But why kill Jax to save the third guy?"

"One, we don't like rats. Two, the third guy was the son of one of our guys."

"Ah, I get it."

"Well, the best I can say is that I didn't tell the cops anything. I told them attorney-client privilege, that was it."

"You better be right because we'll get this from Cap's lawyer."

"I'm not worried. That's what I said."

The three got up and walked over to the corner. They were discussing something animated among themselves.

LEON AND BANKRUPTCY

I had been thinking about Leon's problem with the Germantown properties. Like most lawyers, we know the questions, but we need to look up the answers. I had a pretty good idea of what I wanted to tell him, but I wanted to run it by a real creditor's rights attorney. I called Joe Barson, he had had the office down to the hall from mine and was a decent guy. I had to borrow some of Leon's time on using the phone, but he already had a stash from his underlings in the prison. Joe, like most specialists in an area of the law, doesn't mind being asked questions because they feel the one asking the questions will refer them bigger paying matters when the time comes. Yet they do expect you to have done your homework. They expect a concise relevant statement of facts, and at least a preliminary review of the law. I laid out Leon's problem and my preliminary conclusions. Joe gave me a verbal pat on the back and confirmed what I had been thinking. I had my plan ready for Leon and his Germantown homeowners. I let Leon know I was ready. He told me he wanted Reggie to sit in. I explained that that would break attorney-client privilege. He said he didn't care, but Reggie was a close adviser and he wanted to follow what I said.

In the afternoon, Leon and Reggie walked past the line of people waiting to see me, no one uttered a peep. These guys ruled the place. They walked in and shut the door.

"Reggie, Leon, I think I got a lot for you here." I pulled out my notes to check off a few things.

"First, Leon, I think you're being ripped off. My people tell me that these debts sell for 25 to 50 cents on the dollar from the big banks and credit card companies. They like their money fast and don't want to get into the business of collecting. Since most of these debts are over six months old and some are over a year, my guess is Labrums bought these for about 25 percent of face maybe even 15 percent. So where you paid him $200,000, he was making $150,000 profit. That may be something you can check out if you have some bank sources."

Leon and Reggie looked at each other. Reggie nodded at Leon. "Don't worry, Leon. I got that covered. I got sources." Then turning to me, "Can you get me a list of where these debts come from?"

"Sure, it's right here." I gave him the list Leon gave me earlier. He made a copy and gave me the original back.

"Next step, Leon. Get the $150,000 from Labrum on the note. What he was doing was getting in on this deal for no money.

"You were gonna put up $200,000, he was gonna pay you back $150,000 but only your $50,000 was in on the deal. Of course, someone would have to pay attorney's fees and court costs, but that would be about $1,000 apiece and you were gonna split that. So basically, you got duped into putting up almost all the money and he was gonna skate."

"I don't like that."

"I guess not. That's why you have to force him to repay the $150,000 he owes you on the note. If he doesn't pay after the ninety days, have your lawyer send him a demand letter and if he doesn't pay, enter judgment and get a lien on the properties he does own. My computer search showed he owned about 20 other proprieties in Philadelphia, including his house. So tell your lawyer to get on it."

"Got it."

"Next, it is interesting that most of these debts are from credit cards, and not second mortgages. The difference is that they are not yet liens on real estate. A home equity loan is a lien on real estate, a simple credit card debt is not. What that means is very important. If these people in Germantown, go into bankruptcy court and file a Chapter 13 bankruptcy they don't lose their houses.

"See, in Chapter 13, the court can do two things. It decides what the income of the debtor is and what he can afford to pay. He is then given up to 60 months to make payments to pay off what he can afford. Now, the liens – home equity loans and first mortgages – they stay on the property. They don't get wiped out, but whatever delinquency there is, gets paid off over 60 months. Now here's the beauty part. Anything that's not a lien, gets added into what he can afford to pay. Anything he can't afford to pay gets wiped out. In bankruptcy terms, it means he is "discharged" from those debts. This is like Chapter 11 in bankruptcy except that is for corporations and such. Donald Trump used Chapter 11 to get out of millions in debt with his casinos by showing a loss, so they passed a law to let ordinary people do the same."

"What does this Chapter 13 cost?"

"Between $1,000 and $1,500, usually. But I got you a deal. Normally, I get a one-third referral fee so I can kick that back to you. But I got a guy who will do this for $500 apiece without a referral fee if we refer him at least 20 people."

"So what happens is this. All 40 people file Chapter 13, and pay $500 apiece. They get to save their house and pay off the delinquency and the debts over a 60 month period. But the fee they paid is part of the debt so you get and paid back over 60 months. The money all goes to the debt owners, this Keisha Smallwood will receive whatever the court has ordered the people to pay monthly. So you get a lot of your money back but you'll just have to wait for it, and the people save their homes and wipe out a lot of their debt."

"Whoa. I can do all that."

"I'm sure of it. You have to get some of your people, and to talk to these homeowners and get them started on the Chapter 13 business. There are time limits on this stuff."

"I've got some of my men who will get on it. The people will be happy to hear about it and especially that I did it."

"Atta boy. Lots of win-win all around."

"I like it. What about you, Reggie?"

"Yeah. I follow it, too. Great work, Jake. We owe you big time."

"Well, I don't smoke weed that much."

"No, I got something else in mind. We'll talk."

Leon was already on his illegal mobile phone telling one of his lieutenants what to do.

I called Joe Barson and told him to get ready for about 40 clients for Chapter 13. Labrums wouldn't know what hit him.

"What do I do with the money that these people pay back through Keisha?"

"You keep it."

"But what if he wants his share?"

"You don't give it to him. He won't sue you because he'd be asked what he bought these debts for and it will turn out he defrauded you. The best thing you did was to get Keisha to own the debts. He won't say a word when you keep the money."

"Okay, I like it." He turned to Reggie. Reggie nodded. "Now, I got one more question. What did the Spawn want with you the other day?"

"First, as you may know I had a private consultation with Jax. They wanted to know what that was about. I told them it was confidential, and protected by attorney- client privilege. Then, I was visited by some cops from Chester County and they wanted to know what I discussed with Jax. I also told them that conversation was protected by attorney-client privilege. Dog wanted to know what I said to the cops and if it was about Jax. I told them I couldn't say. They then told me that Jax was involved in a robbery with Cap and another guy. They had already caught Cap and wanted to know if Jax was going to rat out the other guy to save his skin."

"They must have killed Jax, figuring he was gonna rat."

"I would guess that too."

"So that means you could tell the cops who the third guy was if Jax told you."

"If he told me that, I would have no reason to tell them anything. Besides I can always insist on attorney-client privilege."

"They won't believe that. They know everyone in jail trades on information."

"But the Chester cops can't help me. I've been sentenced, my case is on appeal. I'm gonna get max good time when I'm up for parole. What can they give me?"

"We'll see about that. Let me do some digging."

"I'd appreciate that, but there's only so much you can do."

"You'll see."

Reggie spoke up. "Yo, Jake, I like your style. You got me thinking. I have a few ideas. Let's talk in a bit."

"Reggie, I'm always happy to talk."

"Good, see you then."

We got up and went to dinner. At least I was active and employed. The days were passing better now.

Shower Confrontation

It was the end of the day and our time for access to the showers. The bathrooms were a large ancient tile expanse dating back to the 1930s. On one side were a line of sinks and urinals. On the other was a large open room with 10 shower heads. I was walking down to the showers with my soap, shaving kit and towel when, out of a narrow alcove stepped five of the Devil's Spawn including Dog.

"Where you going, Jake?" Dog barked.

"To take a shower."

"Not before we get some answers. What did Jax tell you?"

"Can't say. I told you that." Besides I knew if I said anything I was doomed.

"What did he tell the cops?"

"Nothing. I already told you that."

"We think you need a little persuading." They advanced on me. Somehow, they had a few clubs and a knife. I turned to run back the hall and saw a sea of black faces appear behind me. Big Henry, of course, and Leon/Tariq were recognizable. And I was in the middle. As Big Henry reached me, he pushed me behind him and a group formed around me. Somehow an array of weapons appeared in the hands of the guys with Big Henry – pipes, screw drivers, car aerials, ball point pens, chair legs. Where the hell were the guards? I knew some of the guards sold us grass, but did they ignore the gang fights? I guess they did.

In any case, the black guys advanced with their own assortment of clubs and knives. Dog and his crew couldn't back down now, they had drawn a line. In the macho rules of prison, they couldn't back down or they would become bitches for everyone to pick on. Dog the leader had no diplomatic skills to get out of this one. What happened next was not pretty.

Like two ancient armies, they each advanced on the other and began swinging. Dog was clubbed first on the front of his neck by Big Henry with a broom handle and he fell trying to breathe with his hands at his throat. Henry swatted away a few blows directed at him and then he swung at the ribs of one of the Spawn, dropping him while he clutched at his rib cage. As the Spawn fell, they were beaten around their torsos and legs. Somehow, rules for these fights had evolved. There were to be no killings so death blows to the head were out. Blows to the torso and legs would beget some lengthy hospital time, but very little investigation or punishment. But the Spawn needed to be humiliated for picking on a protected member of another gang. It seems I had been adopted not only by the old black guys, but also by Tariq's black Muslims probably the most feared group. The Spawn were now down the totem pole and would be treated as bitches _____

It only lasted about 10 minutes, but heaps of Spawn lay moaning and gasping on the floor. It was obvious that the areas of choice attack had been the ribs and legs. I could hear bones breaking and snapping in the melee. By the end, there was not a single Spawn standing and most were unconscious. Dog had not moved after the first blow.

The black multitude then quietly with little said walked back up the hall and dispersed, hiding their weapons in their prison jumpsuits.

Almost as if on cue, or actually probably on cue, a few guards went back down the hall to the fallen Spawn. I could hear the radio calls asking for stretchers and gurneys. The Spawn were then wheeled or carried down to the infirmary.

And so it ended, quietly. I could not stop shaking as the adrenalin pumped through my body. Squiffy helped me walk back.

I am a nice white boy from the suburbs. When we have fights, there is a lot of pushing and shoving, a lot of daring each other to take the first punch. No real injuries or attacks. This fight in the hallway was like nothing I had seen or imagined. Brutal blows, no hesitation. These men had been through this their whole lives. Street survival required constant awareness, and instantaneous brutality. I was still shaking for hours after the fight. I could not look at the Spawn mangled and bloody on the floor, not moving, just groans.

CHESTER COUNTY COPS

Early the next morning the cops from Chester County and Montgomery County were interested in the fight. Chester County because that was the home turf of the Spawn, Montgomery County because that was where Graterford Prison was located. It took them two hours of interviews to find out absolutely nothing. No one was talking. Not surprisingly the guards were magically unable to report on a major incident. They simply wanted no part of a confrontation between the Spawn and the Muslims. Maybe the whole thing would disappear in time, and they wouldn't have to do paperwork. Of course, the warden addressed all shifts at lunchtime, and warned us that we all had to cooperate. He knew it was never a possibility, but he knew he had to give the lecture. After the cops re-interviewed the usual suspects, one of the Chester County cops motioned me over for an interview. Maybe, he had pieced together something had been directed at me. I went obediently into the makeshift interview room.

The first cop asked, "What can you tell us? You're not one of these guys, you must know something."

"Even if I did, would I want to end up in the infirmary sharing a room with one of the Spawn? You must know better than that."

"We talked to you before. Is there anything you want to tell us?"

"Is there anything you can do for me? Something worth a few months recuperating from broken bones in the hospital."

I was learning prison ways. Everything had value, nothing was given for free.

"What did you want?"

"Like I told you before. I want a nice long furlough and I want to know how my case got transferred to Judge Hawley. And I want good evidence, the kind I can use in court."

"We're from Chester County. We don't know that stuff."

"If you want my information, you know you can help."

"Is your information good?"

"Pure gold. I guarantee."

"Okay, we'll see what we can do."

"I walked out back to my cell. As I went, I personally thanked Leon and Big Henry. I don't know how they knew what was gonna happen, but they did. That's how prison worked.

Reggie and Leon
Confer on Wealth

It was just after lunch and Reggie and Leon wanted to confer with me. They said they had a number of things to discuss. One thing was getting to be very apparent. Both of these men had not been raised in the white culture, but both had prodigious intellects when it came to social skills and abstract ideas. I have no idea what might have become of them if they had middle class parents and gone to suburban high schools. Conversations with them were always enlightening. It was amazing how they observed the American culture and were able to manipulate it to their benefit.

Reggie was the first to speak when he described his prior two arrests for fraud. Reggie had dropped out of high school in eleventh grade, but managed to take community college courses in computers and banking. He wrote at an eight grade level, but could speak in intelligent terms with a few grammatical lapses; yet at the same time he could revert to the language of the streets in Ebonics without missing a beat. When not in prison, he could dress in the latest fashion without appearing gaudy or overstated. He had an original wife and two "Muslim wives" all of whom he supported in a decent manner. Two of the wives had borne his children and one – a recent acquisition – had a nice apartment and a position as a receptionist in a high level corporate office. One thing Reggie was good at was defrauding banks and, while he was serving the second of two prison terms he had apparently laundered and stashed his money.

His first fraud was an invention out of his own head. He had discovered that many large business organizations never reconcile their checking accounts on a monthly basis, i.e. they do not balance their deposits against the checks they have written because I guess, it is a massive job. So by maintaining contacts with a few of the female clerks in the various banks, he could determine which customers maintained high balances in their accounts. He would then obtain copies of the customers' checks, reproduce copies on the computer, complete with the color of the checks, and the account numbers and the type face of the printing. He could then obtain ink stamps of the signatures on the checks. Again through his wooing of female clerks in the banks, he would set up a totally bogus corporate account at several banks and deposit his newly written checks into his own bogus account. From this account, he would write out checks of less than $10,000 payable to dozens of homeless, poor or deadbeat people who would deposit them into accounts newly created for them. On the appointed day, several of Reggie's lieutenants would escort these people to the banks on the day after their checks cleared and have them withdraw just under $10,000 which is the amount that draws scrutiny from the federal agencies tracking money laundering. The people would then keep $3,000, his lieutenants would keep $2,000 and he would have delivered to him just under $5,000 in cash. So three days a week, Reggie would receive nearly $5,000 from 40 accounts delivered to his house. He would do this for four weeks and shut down the operation and start up again a month later. The corporate checks he had written might bounce several months later when Reggie's bogus check was discovered, and then the individual checks would be discovered to be derived from a massive fraud scheme. The only identifiable participants in the scheme were poor, homeless, unemployed people. Their crime was to participate in a scheme to pass a bad check of under $10,000 – a minor misdemeanor barely worth prosecuting. Eventually, the bank detectives arrested a few of them and got them to identify Reggie's lieutenants, but the lapse of time, the difficulty of identifying the lieutenants caused most of the investigations to founder.

Unfortunately for Reggie, his lieutenants either got greedy or proved to be unreliable. Some were arrested on other charges and gave up Reggie's scheme to cut down on their sentences. Some tried to duplicate Reggie's scheme without his finesse and discipline and got caught. However, because the scheme involved so much paperwork, so many people, so much documentary evidence, the bank detectives, the FBI and the local prosecutors could simply not get their acts together. They let Reggie plead guilty in a negotiated plea for three years.

Unfortunately, he ran two more scams from jail and again got caught by unreliable lieutenants. But Reggie seemed happy in prison life. He was immediately accorded a high rank in the prestige system. Also, he was given regular furloughs and weekends off. I don't know how, but most of the guards were always happy to greet him. I never knew the system for getting passes for weekends or furloughs. Maybe, I hadn't been in prison long enough to earn a reputation or acquire the knowledge to negotiate a temporary release. Reggie did. Somehow, he was able to visit his original wife, or one of his Muslim wives and bring nice presents. The appropriate wife for that weekend would be waiting at the prison entrance in a new car for him. I never asked, and was never told, but everyone seemed to recognize his exalted status in the system.

BUSINESS CHAT WITH
LEON AND REGGIE

It was a slow day for me to interview my "clients" so Leon and Reggie came to my computer room without a computer for a chat.

"Jake," said Leon, "we've been wondering about a few things. See, black folks never have much of a background in managing money, we don't have rich uncles or trustworthy lawyers or businessmen we can count on to handle our money if we ever get it. Now, we both trust and like you – so here's the question, what do we do with our money? We both have a good bit stashed."

"Guys, I told you before, I can't tell you how to launder money gotten illegally."

"No, no, we know that. It's all legal money now, sitting in bank accounts, and brokerage accounts in different names. All legal."

"Well, I can't tell you how to protect it from creditors."

"No, no, we got all that – joint name with wife, trust for kids, corporate name – no we got all that. How do we invest it?"

"I see. Well, I'm not an expert on finances, but I can tell you what rich people do, and don't do."

"Something like that."

"First, avoid the stock market. All I see are slick guys in fancy suits trying to sell you something that a bunch of suits in New York tell them to sell to clients are too small to get anyone's attention. Little guys in the stock market get slaughtered. So forget that.

"Real estate is usually pretty good if you can actually control it yourself. Buying in with partners usually leads to a dispute or mismanagement. But if you can keep an eye on it yourself, it can be good."

"One problem with real estate is cycles. It seems our economy goes through cycles based on inflation and lots of other unknown factors. We seem to go through periods where the economy is stagnant, and periods when we have a boom. In real estate, or even in the stock market, when we were in a stagnant or down period, relax, don't try to do anything, don't row against the current. These periods seem to last about seven years give or take. Then we go through boom periods, when everyone is a winner. As we say, inflation floats all boats. Then put your money to work. The best place then is real estate because of leverage. You can borrow up to 70 percent to buy investment real estate. So if the rest of the economy goes up 10 percent, the 70 percent you borrowed does not. So if the whole asset goes up 10 percent your investment goes up to 40 percent or a 400 percent gain. This is an oversimplification, but it seems we have seven lean years followed by seven flat years."

"Wow. Never heard that before!"

"Real estate is good, but it isn't what we call liquid. It may not sell so fast when you need money. It' is difficult to buy because you have to jump through hoops to get a mortgage and you have to inspect it very thoroughly. But in the long run, for a guy who doesn't need the money right away, and can last through the down periods, it works well."

Reggie asked, "I can't put anything in my name and I have no credit. How do I handle that?"

"First, you put the property in a corporate name or in trust for your kid. Or you set up a limited partnership. You'll need a decent lawyer for that. I used to do this all the time. Then you pay people to apply for the mortgage. After the boom is on the property, they transfer it to you."

"Got it. So seven lean years, seven fat years."

"When you get out, can you handle all this for us?"

"Sure. It's second nature to me."

We then went into a lengthy discussion about neighborhoods around Philly. They only understood ghetto finances, but big real estate deals were a mystery. Suburban apartments, shopping centers, office buildings. They wanted to learn it all. It was like teaching a college course, but this time my class was paying attention, and sucked up every detail. They weren't out at a kegger looking to get lucky, they were here to learn. I went through ways to calculate numbers, return on investment leverages, inflation indicators, risk factors. They took it all in. And you know, the more I taught the more I learned myself. When you educate a person who has no preconceptions about your subject and he asks a question, you reexamine the whole conversational body of wisdom and learn it from scratch. These little seminars were getting my mind to work again. My self-pitying funk was lifting.

Reggie on the Road

At dinner that night, Reggie swung by the old black guys' table, and said "Jake, meet me after breakfast tomorrow. Meet me at the cell block D 7:00 a.m. sharp." He didn't say more. What was up? Who knew? I didn't get a chance to ask and no one at the table mentioned it. They weren't going to get into Reggie's business, but somehow they knew something was up. So I waited until breakfast the next day and then met Reggie.

At the door to the cell block, Reggie met me and led me past the door as the guards opened first the one door by the electronic lock, as it shut behind us, they opened the second door. As it swung shut behind us, Reggie led me down to the administrative corridor of the prison. Waiting for us there, were our civilian clothes in a pile next to our wire baskets. Following Reggie's silent lead, we changed into our civilian clothes and put on prison jumpsuits in the wire basket. We went to the next window, and were handed $30 in cash which we signed for and Reggie drew $100 out of his commissary account. I followed Reggie wordlessly out of the prison, past the guards to the parking lot. Reggie got behind the wheel of the prison truck and I got in the passenger side. I still had no idea what was up but somehow I had been released from prison.

As we got to the end of the long prison driveway and turned left on Route 113 to go to Route 422, Reggie spoke up.

"We got a pickup to make. The rototiller for the garden was on the fritz so we're gonna pick it up from the repair shop"

"Uh-huh. But, Reggie, we're on our own. No guards. Can't we run away? Do they trust us?"

"I got you upgraded to trustee."

"But I've only been here a few months."

"Don't ask. I got it done."

"Oh, I see. So we're gonna pick up a rototiller."

"Yup. We got eight hours to get to Reading and back."

"But, Reading is only 45 minutes away, maybe less."

"Yup."

"But we got a day's meal money."

"Yup."

"So we gonna do something else."

"Yup. Reggie looked over at last with a sly smile on his face. "Yes, we are."

"Ah-ha! So I have to wait to find out?"

"Yup." Again he smiled.

We got the rototiller about 9:00 as the hardware shop was opening and put it in the back of the truck and lashed it down so it wouldn't roll around.

Then Reggie drove up to an older shopping center on the outskirts of Reading and pulled up to the "Lucky Spa." I followed Reggie in the door as he was greeted by a plump older black lady wrapped in a scarlet silk robe and a big smile.

"Reggie. How you been?"

"Great, Nitsy, great. And I got lotsa time and a friend. We want the best."

"I got nothing else. You know that."

"My friend here is on my ticket, so treat him well."

"You know you got no ticket here. You is an honored guest." She gave him a big hug and led him to a small mirror on the wall. Reggie motioned me over to look into the mirror. As I got close, I could see through the mirror to the other side. Four women were sitting on an array of couches and armchairs in an assortment of lingerie. There were two pretty Asian girls, a white one and a black one. They were looking at the mirror on their side and knew someone was looking at them. They put down their coffees and primped a bit for us.

"So, Jake, what you like?" Reggie spoke. I felt that with two black people in the room, I should not make the choice they expected, so I picked the black girl. She was slim and pretty in a teal silk robe, with a nice royal blue set of bra and panties.

"Reggie, I'll take the one in the blue bra and panties."

"Excellent choice, Jake. You ain't a man till you dipped your pen in ink." He and Nitsy guffawed and slapped each other on the back. "If you ain't done it before, you better be ready for something else."

I blushed, betraying my lack of experience in cultural diversity while they treated me like a college freshman on his first encounter. More laughs, more jokes about the sexual prowess of the African race.

Nitsy finally showed me the door down the hallway to meet the girl she referred to as Laura Mae. Fortunately, Nitsy knew well what men liked and had selected Laura Mae, not because she was thin and had the arms and legs of a sparrow, but was full backed and strong. She had these marvelous buttocks and thighs that her race was amply endowed with.

As Laura Mae led me down the corridor in the half light, she took my arm and cuddled into me. "So, Jake, is it? We're gonna have some fun." I have to admit I was having a few misgivings. When I had selected a black woman, I meant it both as a tribute to my new found friends in the Old Black Guys Gang and as a polite gesture to Reggie and Nitsy for their hospitality. But was I being politically incorrect and obvious to have as my first commercial experience a black prostitute. Was I rewriting racial stereotypes? This was my first commercial venture into the sensual arts and I was afraid my conflict might put the fear of guilt into my precious little member and limit his usual lusty performance.

We stripped and I was led into a shower where I was given a thorough – I mean thorough – soaping not only to my upper body but to my nether regions as well and I mean all my nether regions. Not wishing to be ungrateful or remiss in my obligations, I soaped Laura Mae equally as thoroughly. I was delighted that this experience left me amply rampant not to say, at stately full salute. I was toweled and rubbed with a body crème equally as thoroughly as in the shower. From the shower, we reclined on a large bed. I lingered, as did she, over some of the finer blandishments accompanied by mutual heavy breathing and a few animal grunts. She mounted me expertly and sucked me up into her smoothly and easily. As I approached the acme of sexual release, she would slide into another position and reinstate a wonderful rhythm. Our play seemed to last for hours, when at last, I could hold out no longer and delivered a thundering burst and a mighty roar. We lay panting and exhausted bathed in sweat. After a few minutes, she got up and, with a warm wash cloth, wiped me down. Easily, she was a virtuoso and plied her trade with the touch of a master. Perhaps, I am exaggerating because of my length time without feminine companionship but the art of love while venerated in ancient pagan times had fallen into disrepute. I was imagining what might happen if we had international competitions and awarded something akin to the World Cup or the Pulitzer Prize. No. I guess my long deprivation was talking. I went back up the corridor and was greeted by Reggie and Nitsy with big smiles. Laura Mae came up with my jacket and held it up for me to put on.

Laura Mae had another big smile, "White boy did good!" Of course this was welcomed with many guffaws and back slappings by Reggie and Nitsy. I could only blush. Reggie and I waved as we left.

"Thanks, Reggie."

"You my man, Jake. You take care of me and I take care of you. Now how about a steak for lunch." I could see that was part of Reggie's routine.

"Sounds great." My recent exertion and the prison diet suggested no other, even for lunch. We pulled up at an Outback on Route 22 and ordered steaks, baked potatoes and a couple of draft beers. Reggie got his well-done, mine was medium rare. As soon as it was served, the meals vanished in what seemed like seconds.

In the meantime, Reggie timed me with a serious look on his face. "Jake, you're a good guy. You sound like you got set up and I want to help. Now, you got to tell me everything from the beginning and let me see what I can do. You been good to the brothers and I can be good in return."

So I reiterated my tale of woe. The letter of our firm's stationary with my boss' signature telling the brokerage firm to redirect the $3.1 million wire to a new phony account set upon the firm's name. How the lady assistant vice president Hollister had supposedly identified me as the one setting up the account. How the bank's cameras had not captured the transaction. How the wire had come in and then a wire forwarded the money to a Cayman Islands bank account and the trail had grown cold from there. How we had requested to see bank accounts of several of the lawyers in the firm and that of the lady assistant vice president and been denied. How I had waived a jury trial, and then how the trial judge had been replaced by Judge Hawley, who not only found me guilty but denied me bail. As we spoke, my appeal was pending and would not be heard for several more months if not a few years. Reggie listened carefully and occasionally asked a few questions to clarify. He seemed to know the law well and was careful in getting details of my story straight. He sat for a few minutes staring off into space while I took another sip of beer.

After a few sips of beer, Reggie started, "I can see we need a few things that it is within my ability to deliver. First, we need all the bank accounts for the members of your law firm. Not only their bank accounts, but also their credit card accounts and their home mortgage and home equity accounts. One flaw in their operation was that most of your old firm does business exclusively with their client, Franklin National. Obviously, they would fight tooth and nail to avoid giving you access to those accounts and the judge cooperated by denying you access. The identity of those who set you up is in those accounts. I am sure that they have gotten some of the money back from the Cayman Island accounts in small enough wires to avoid attracting attention. So first things first, we get copies of all bank accounts, credit card statements, home mortgages and home equity accounts at Franklin National."

"But, Reggie, my firm has over 150 lawyers."

"Start by narrowing the list. Eliminate the lawyers younger than you. Include everyone who could be involved in municipal bond financing, include everyone who you knew and worked closely with, including everyone under, let's say 40, and eliminate those who you think could not possibly be involved. Let's try for a list of 25."

"Okay, but how can you do this?"

"Leave that to me. I've got sources."

"Can you get the accounts for this lady?"

"No sweat. Leave it to me."

"Okay. Next," Reggie continued. "I want all investigative notes on this lady. I want everything on her, good, bad or indifferent. I want her relatives, her finances, her lovers, I want it all. And then I'm going to do my own thing."

"The lady has to be in on it. Someone had to disable the bank camera. That doesn't happen by itself. Someone had to slip in a new CD or disable it. I suspect a new CD. If we can get it we got our case. I'm sure the lady got some money out of this.

"I also suspect that the brokerage firm may have been in on it. Get me the name of the contacts for the bond financing. They must have gotten some money back from this deal. I need the name of his bank, too. I'll get all his accounts."

"I'll also get Hawley's accounts from his bank. He might have got something.

"Believe me, bank contacts I got. No one suspects the lower people at the banks know as much as they do. But they have access to information you wouldn't believe. And they get paid shit. A little sugar goes a long way and Reggie's got the sugar."

"My god, Reggie, can you do all this?"

"Consider it done."

After lunch, we drove the truck to a pleasant hillside at a small town park outside Collegeville, and took a nap on the bank for a while. I drifted off to sleep thinking of all the things I might need to re-examine my case. For the first time in months I had hope. We drifted back to the prison about 4:00 p.m. and unloaded the rototiller by the garden shed and signed back in. We took off our civilian clothes and put back on the orange prison jump suits. It wasn't dinner time yet, so I ran back to my cell, pulled out my file and got the list of my firm's lawyers. I whittled the list down to 25 and handed it to Reggie at dinner. He faxed the list to his lawyer with instructions to forward it to one of his lieutenants. Prison mail is extremely restricted. Letters come in and go out only to certain people on a predetermined list, usually close relatives. Only mail to lawyers was not read or censored so everything went in and out as legal mail if it was sensitive. The matter was now in Reggie's hands. Could he really do anything or was this just a con?

SATCHEL

Satchel's release to the halfway house had come through, but typical of the prison system, it took a few days to process his paperwork. The guard came down midmorning and handed Satchel his papers. It was a big day for celebration. Satchel picked up his belongings in a cardboard box and walked through the cell block to high-fives, cheers, and the usual good natured taunts. He was all smiles as he left through the double-locked doors, down the administrative corridor and out the front gate. Some of his friends had come to pick him up and drive him to the halfway house in North Philadelphia.

I now had the cell to myself, but was expecting a transfer soon. This would be my chance to gauge what the guards and the warden thought of me. Of course, I had been given trustee status when I went out with Reggie to pick up the rototiller, and I was helping a few of the men out with legal advice. What the warden would decide now would be interesting. I went with my usual crew to dinner and was handed a message that the assistant warden wanted to see me. I guessed this was good news.

After dinner, I went to the assistant warden's office and was waved in when I stood at his glass paneled door.

"Ah, Mr. Jacobson. Please have a seat." The assistant warden was not an ex-cop, or an ex-guard, he had a degree in psychology and government. This was a good sign. "Mr. Jacobson, you have a positive effect on our men with your legal counseling. It helps them understand the system."

"Thank you, Sir." The assistant warden, Mr. Miller, was a plump, rather homely man with wispy curly hair and a pair of horn-rimmed glasses on a jowly face. He enjoyed a decent reputation among the men and seemed friendly enough. He also enjoyed the fact that he had control over a large group of possibly dangerous men.

"Mr. Jacobson. We would like you to teach some courses for the man."

"What sort of courses?"

"Law and Criminal Procedure obviously, and maybe American History."

"Well, I've had those courses, but I've never taught before and I'd need text and study materials."

"We already have them from past classes. If you'd study them over, and let me know if they are helpful. People have tried this before, but were not well received.

"I could do that."

"If you do, we would grant you full trustee status. Right now, you were on probationary status. We also may let you teach at one of the prisons in Berks, or Delaware County, depending on enrollment."

"Okay, so far."

"Now the pay is not great. As a prisoner you would get $1.37 per hour paid into your commissary account."

"Be still my heart! What would I do with all that money?"

"I know, I know. Regulations prevent us paying prisoners more."

"No. I understand. I might like that. Can you send materials around?"

"Sure. And, you get a cell in the trustee wing." That meant a nicer cell, much smaller, but all to myself. I get not only a bed with box springs instead of an army double decker with questionable springs.

"Do I give grades? Is this for credit?"

"Not yet, it depends on whether we get you accredited. You have a JD degree, but you haven't taken any education courses, but sometimes that accrediting bodies waive those. So, no grades, no credit just yet."

BANK RECORDS

It took ten days for Reggie's source to come through. At lunch I was handed a note from one of the guards that there was a package waiting for me in the mailroom. I went down as soon as I could, any mail is a big event, but this could be huge. I saw three boxes of file paper stacked in the corner, all marked with the stamp of "Legal Mail." This meant a confidential communication with my lawyer and not subject to prison review or censorship. The office lent me a hand truck to take the boxes back to my cell. I couldn't stand the anticipation of the chance to examine the banking accounts of my firm, colleagues and the lady from the bank. I was hoping against hope that there was some gold, some glint, some buried evidence which could help me. I saw that each box contained in separate folders neatly sorted first, the checking account records, second the credit and debit card accounts, third the mortgage and home equity accounts for 25 of my firm members and the bank lady.

Since the bank lady was the most obvious, I sorted out her piles first and went through them. In the third month after the $3.1 million disappeared she started to get $15,000 a month wired into her account. This went on for months. Someone didn't want to have her get all the money at once so she wouldn't be tempted to spend it all at once and attract attention. If we only knew this at the time of trial, but we were blocked by the bank's lawyers and the District Attorney with Judge Hawley's help. Ms. Hollister was careful, she paid off her credit cards, then her home equity, then she opened a brokerage account. As each monthly check came in, she was very prudent and distributed each payment over all of her debts first.

The amounts weren't very big. She was fairly shrewd and conservative. I highlighted each important transaction.

I then decided to check out my boss' account, Ivan Gardner. Mainly, I just wanted to see what he made and get a little personal dirt on him. I was shocked to see a similar pattern of distributions to him. On the third month, he also got $25,000 into his checking account, but he also got $5,000 wired into his credit card account, $5,000 his home equity account and $5,000 his home mortgage. When the credit cards and home equity were paid off, there was an extra $20,000 going into his checking account. From there, he put money into a brokerage account. So, he was taking back $40,000 per month. I was shocked as I went through Gardner's records that he was in on it. We had worked closely together for several years and he had been my boss. Was I threatening to him? Did he do this to get rid of me as competition? He was up for partner soon, did he think I might interfere with his plans? But mainly, I was surprised that someone I knew for frequent daily contact could bring himself to do something this evil, and to me. I highlighted each of his transactions over the past months. He had been very circumspect with money – getting out of debt first, in small unobtrusive amounts and then stashing the money in brokerage accounts. Smart… Careful. But I also knew Gardner. He was not capable of planning this himself. He simply didn't have the balls. He was a nitpicker, a guy who covered his ass, he wore a belt and suspenders. He had to have been lead by someone devious. I looked at the rest of the 24 piles, someone was in there. I had been lucky with the first two. The rest would be drudgery, but at least I had the relevant dates and the pattern. When I got there, I would know. In the meantime, I was careful to send copies of the pages of the accounts to my lawyer. I didn't want anything to disappear and I didn't want to give anyone an excuse to get rid of me. The evidence would still be there. So then each day, I plodded through the rest of the accounts. First, the municipal financing people – no help. Then, the lawyers who dealt most with Franklin National – no help. Still, 14 to go.

CHATSWORTH

After plowing through mounds of bank records, I finally came to a partner whose deposits into his accounts occurred about the same time as Gardner's – Christopher Chatsworth. He was a junior partner in the litigation department, about five years older than Gardner, and eight older than I. Sure enough, he had $25,000 going into his checking account, but he had a massive credit card debt from four different cards, so $40,000 was distributed equally among them.

Chatsworth was one of the last people I would have suspected. He was a funny, engaging kind of guy with a pretty debutante wife, a family with high up society connections and a solid future as a litigator with the firm. He was in his early forties, wore straight Ivy League suits, ties, shoes and belonged to the best golf and tennis club in the right part of town. One of the guys with a decent personality and the ability to attract clients. Why would someone like that risk engaging in criminal activity? What was his connection with Gardner – a dull, grinding nerd? He clearly was taking an equal amount and was in on it with him somehow.

I completed the rest of the bank statements over the next several days and found no other similar patterns of deposits into the accounts. _____.

Of course, there might be more, but at least I knew who needed to be investigated. I found Reggie and Leon sitting against the wall watching the basketball game in the yard.

"Reggie, I maybe got something to show you when you get a chance."

"Sure, Jake. Let's try after lunch."

"Sure thing!"

* * *

I was sitting in my "office" the deserted computer room when Reggie and Leon came in. I had laid out the bank records for my three suspects and had bright-lined the important entries. Each month had been separately paper-clipped and each page with significant entries had a colored tab.

Reggie looked at his pile. "Very nice, counselor. Very nice." Leon looked over another pile and followed the entries.

"Unfortunately it's not conclusive evidence. I mean I know, but to prove it in court is another thing. Some $3.1 million went missing and large sums going out to each of the main conspirators each month, I know they did it, but it's just circumstance, not proof beyond a reasonable doubt and not enough evidence even for me to get a new trial."

"Hmmm… wait a minute, there, Jake." Leon mumbled as he looked over Chatsworth's records. Hmm. First, I see him spending a lot of money on his credit cards. I know these accounts. They're whore houses and lots of sexual activity. I see one in particular I have an interest in. The Petronius Club. This is a private club for rich guys – they drink, snort coke and do expensive women. Very expensive. It's a group that meets every two weeks for an orgy. My buddy, Patsy runs it. He's Italian, connected with the mob but he gets his coke from one of my guys. He passes himself off as "Antoine La Violet" – a French nobleman. He's got a serious crowd of rich guys who control who gets in and who doesn't."

"Can he help me with this?"

"Sure, Patsy and I go back a long way, but we can't fuck up his gig. Only Chatsworth."

"No. I get it. Just get Chatsworth, then squeeze him. Great."

"Let me work on that. I'll get something."

Meanwhile, Reggie picked up his head. "You know, Jake, you got something else here, too."

"What's that?"

"You see these numbers on the statements. They're all the same – nine digits."

"What do they mean?"

"They're bank routing numbers. But they're not American numbers."

"What does that mean?"

"It means we can identify where this money came from, what bank."

"I see. Well, I can identify the bank the $3.1 million wire went into in the Caymans. If it matches, that means the money went into and came out of the same bank."

"Yes... Yes. That's it. A bit more proof. And I'll tell you something else. I got connections in the Caymans. Maybe, we can link up the deposits and withdrawals. I got girl friends who got access. Now it's gotta be hush hush, but they can't testify, but at least we know we're on the right track."

"Got it. Thanks, guys. No kidding. I'm very grateful. Anything you need, just ask."

"Leon mumbled. "We owe you anyway, but we'll get along fine."

While I had the answers, I still had to figure out how to ask the questions. The bank records had been concealed from me before by the court, by refusing my motion for discovery. If I had the documents I wanted and had introduced them at my trial, it certainly could have raised reasonable doubt in the minds of the jurors. Especially Ms. Hollister. But the records I now had might not actually prove my innocence. It might just be a coincidence that these three people were receiving large funds from the same bank the $3.1 million had been deposited in. A very suspicious coincidence. Unfortunately the legal standard to get a new trial once I had been convicted was high. There must be show to exist evidence which could not have been known at the time of the original trial despite the exercise of the diligence and would result in an acquittal, not just suspicion.

At least we now knew the conspirators who had set me up. I would have to figure how to get to them, to expose their guilt possibly to get a confession. But I was stuck in jail, had no funds. Nonetheless, I made a copy of the bank records and sent them to my lawyer for safe keeping.

Patsy Petronius

It took a few days, but Leon stopped me in the hallway on my way to lunch. "Yo, Jake. Reggie got it arranged. You and I are taking the truck to transport stuff to Chester County Prison. We're gonna meet Patsy."

"No shit. How does he do that?"

"Don't ask. Just say thank you." I could see Reggie looking at us from down the hallway. I gave him the thumbs up sign. He nodded. I wasn't sure we were doing something illegal, but I had no choice. These two guys could save my life. I wasn't sure what I had done for them was enough, but I didn't ask.

I had another unusual sign. As I was walking to the administrative wing, I saw the Vice Warden coming the other way. He nodded to me, "Keep up the good work, Mr. Jacobson," he said. Whoa, what was that all about? I remembered, "Don't ask." This Reggie was a magician.

Anyway, the next day, Leon and I left in the prison truck loaded with a number of things for Chester County Prison – records, some of our vegetables, an old desktop copier – all included on a manifest.

Once again, we had been allotted eight hours to complete an errand that took two hours at most. Leon drove us to an old tap room in Chester. This was a beat up old tavern in the heart of downtown Chester. It was still morning so a few customers mostly black were either drinking at the bar, or sitting at tables drinking coffee. It was an amazement to me, but the guys at the bar were drinking beer, and I could see a few shot glasses. What were they doing drinking at this hour?" As we peered through the haze of cigarette smoke and our eyes adjusted to the dimly lit room, we could see an older white guy sitting at the rear table. He was counting receipts, and tabs and had a pile of cash in neat stacks in front of him.

Leon spoke first, "Are you Patsy?"

"Who's asking?" He didn't' look up.

"Tariq." His eyes shot up.

"Tariq! Sure, sure, good to see you. Sorry didn't' recognize you at first."

"Patsy, I got a friend here that needs a favor. His name is Jake."

"Sure, sure, sit down."

Patsy was a nice looking, well-groomed man in his 50s. His hair was very full, and black with silver streaks at the sides. He was wearing what we called the Italian tuxedo – a black and red velour warmup suit unzipped in the front to reveal a white tank top. Hanging from his neck was a large crucifix – I don't mean a cross, I mean a crucifix – Jesus, head askew, with a crown of thorns and all. As we sat, Patsy scooped up the piles of dollar bills and wrapped them in paper wrapper and slid them into his briefcase at his feet. He drew lines where he had stopped counting on the numbers sheet, and looked up.

"Tariq!" Not Leon, not here. Here he was Tariq Shabazz a major drug dealer. "How'd you get out? No… Wait… Don't answer. So what's up?"

"I need some help for my friend."

"Yeah, yeah, so you said. By the way, you like this place? A dump, huh. But a very profitable dump. We do horses, sports and numbers outa here. Ya know the cops never raid black bars so we're good here. But no drugs. The drug cops don't care they bust you just for the stats. Well anyway, what you got?"

"We got something with the Petronius Club, Downtown Philly."

"Sure… Sure… One of mine. What about it? It's a private club for rich guys. They got their own keys, we serve a very nice setup and we got private rooms for them and the girls. We bring in all sorts of girls and make the guys happy. Very classy place, very clean, decorated, ya know. We're open Wednesdays and Fridays only and only after 6:00 p.m. We serve fine Italian food, decent wine. The guys pay monthly to join. They select their own members just so I get my nut. It's located in a rehabbed mansion in West Philly near the Drexel campus. It is all private. Rear entrance Parking lot. But not far from Thirtieth Street Station so the guys can get home to their wives on the Main Line. Very fancy. Hush-hush. Got it?"

"Well, I know somehow we supply you with coke."

"Not me. You don't supply me. You supply them. I make the call to your guy in West Philly and they pick it up from him. I don't touch it. The drug thing is all on them."

"Who picks up the coke?"

"One of their members. It varies. They tell me who, he meets one of your guys and buys a ki usually. Your guy sends me a yard once in a while for the referral."

"They use a whole ki?"

"No… not in one night. Someone takes it home with them. When they run out, they tell me and I set up the buy."

"Got it. Sounds good." A ki was a kilo of cut cocaine, 2.2 pounds of about 50 percent to 80 percent pure coke – cut 50 percent or more with some other powered, usually vitamin B. These guys were doing some serious snorting on their Wednesdays and Fridays and going back to their fancy respectable homes on the upscale Main Line – Wayne, Devon, Villanova, Radnor and voting Republican.

"Look, Patsy, my friend Jake here was screwed by one of the guys here. He got set up so that it looked like he stole $3 million from his law firm. He couldn't beat the rap so now he's doing time out at Graterford with me. We need to set this guy up so he will fess up to setting up Jake here. I know the guys buy from us at 52nd and Baltimore Avenue, so I know who sells to them. We need to catch this guy with some dope on him."

"Sorry, Tariq. No can do. He might ruin my whole operation if you set him up. He's not savvy enough to get through interrogation and he might rat us out to get off himself."

"Do the club members know who they buy from?"

"No. One of your guys. Not always the same makes the sale?"

"Where?"

"In the parking lot of the Wawa. Car to car. About 5:00 p.m. under the lights, but not in the cameras."

"Then he drives to Petronius."

"Yeah, probably. Unless he rakes off some for himself."

"So he's got it in the car."

"Yeah."

"Is he packing?" (Was he carrying a gun?)

"Probably. I would with $20,000 in coke in my front seat."

"How do you know he is doing the pickup?"

"They tell me and I tell your guy."

"That day?"

"Usually, sometimes sooner."

"So you say they don't do a whole ki in one night?"

"Nah. They'd all be dead. There's about 20 to 30 of them."

"So there's maybe about half a ki and a gun in the car."

"Could be."

"Do you know one of the guys name of Chris Chatsworth."

"Sure. He's the treasurer. He pays the bills."

"Does he ever pick up and deliver?"

"About half the time."

"No shit. He has coke in his car?"

"Yup."

"Now, he doesn't leave the left over coke at your club, he takes it home on Wednesdays or Fridays after the club closes."

"Yup."

"Now, if he gets arrested on the way home. He won't' know who tipped him off."

"Maybe."

"But he's not gonna rat out the club and spoil the fun for his buddies."

"Maybe not."

"Besides, you don't touch the dope."

"No. I most certainly do not."

"So he has to rat out his buddies, but not you."

"Yeah. I can see that."

"I mean if he got picked up on the way to the club, he might think my man set him up. But if he gets picked upon the way home, he can only think his buddies or someone else set him up. And it could be any one of 20 or 30 buddies."

"Or me."

"Yeah. That's true."

"Patsy. Now, I gotta ask. Will you let us know when Chatsworth is taking the stuff home, on which night and at what time?"

"Am I talking to cops or am I talking to you?"

"My guy. Send him a text message and he sends it to the cops."

"Yeah, I guess I could do that! What's in it for us?"

"One half free ki delivered when and where you want."

I had to hold my breath. Leon was giving this guy a $10,000 number. That was worth $50,000 to $100,000 on the street. But wholesale $10,000.

"Sure... Sure... Done deal. I send a text message to some guy who doesn't know me in West Philly and he calls the cops on this guy Chatsworth on the way home. And I get a half ki."

"That's it. You in."

"I'm in. You want a beer or something." It was about 11:00 a.m. Not my drinking time. We passed, got back into the truck and made one delivery to the Chester County Prison by 12:00 noon and had the rest of the day free.

"Thanks, Leon. Half a ki. That's a lot. I owe you big time."

"Look, if you win this, you pay me back. If Chatsworth comes, you win. Besides I don't like the guy already. I want to squash him like a big bug on a windshield."

"Yeah. Me too. But thanks."

We rode for a while in silence. I had a lot of planning to do. It was not enough to get Chatsworth arrested and have him admit his guilt. He had to admit what he did to me. Now in federal court when someone pleads, they are required to spill the beans on every crime they are asked about. They cannot do what was known in the Nixon era as a limited hangout. If Chatsworth got asked, he had to tell about the $3 million.

As Tariq explained most drug dealers had connections with some branch of some narc activity. In return for a little protection, the bigger dealers would feed information as "confidential informants" – called CIs to the cops. The cops might be DEA, FBI, local county cops, the Attorney General's detectives. Every one needed stats – a regular history of arrests of dealers so they would avoid arresting the big guys if they got thrown a few bones here and there. It was a particularly good way to get rid of dealers who had crossed them, competitors or just plain guys that pissed them off. So most arrests had information from a CI. In order to protect the sources of cops, the judges would not allow inquiries into who these CIs were. As long as the cop could testify that the CI had provided reliable information in the past that was enough. Of course they couldn't lie so they kept records of the cases in which the CIs provided information. If ever asked, they could reveal their records to the Internal Affairs Division – a group of cops who investigated other cops for bad acts. The bottom line was that the CIs never appeared in court, and their identity was never disclosed. Tariq a/k/a Leon was a well-documented CI.

As Tariq patiently explained: Now each agency had its own CIs and didn't make their lists known to other agencies. This created a royal screw-up. One agency might protect a dealer and his network while another agency might set him up for an arrest and bring him down. As Leon explained, he got caught in the middle of the DEA and the local cops. The locals arrested several of his dealers and they began to roll over on Tariq. When the locals got enough, they arrested him and held a massive grand jury in Philadelphia County and took down Tariq and his guys. Of course, word got around to Tariq that certain people were the local CIs. A few of them turned out to be very bad witnesses. Who knew that would happen? But enough shit stuck to Tariq and he got five years, but he still ran his operation from prison and dropped a few names to the DEA on a regular basis. The DEA had Tariq on their speed dial, but he was in a state prison not a federal one so they couldn't help him much. But he could help them pad their stats from information he got from his people who always had their ears tuned for scuttlebutt. Bottom line: The DEA owed Tariq, but the locals did not...

We had a nice steak lunch at the Capital Grille in King of Prussia after we took 202 North. The waiters seemed to know Tariq and they put us outside. We split a Chateaubriand with béarnaise sauce for two, and a half bottle of terrific red. We got back in the truck. After that meal I could hardly keep my eyes open, so Leon drove back up 422 and 113 to Graterford. We delivered a few items back from Chester County Prison and parked the truck, signed some forms and checked in. The new vice warden nodded cheerfully as we walked down the administrative wing. I took a long luxurious nap. End of a good day.

GARDNER AND
HOLLISTER CAMPAIGNS

While I now knew that Ivan Gardner and Hollister had received wires in substantial amounts of money on a regular basis from the same Cayman Islands bank into which $3.1 million had been wired and that almost certainly meant that they were in on the embezzlement and fraud which had put me in jail, I needed more. The biggest problem was to explain how I had gotten their bank records in the first place, I could not reveal Reggie's source.

I know that if I subpoenaed the records, I would certainly get them at a trial or as part of an investigation, but I had to persuade some government official to get off his (or her) butt and begin an investigation. The records would certainly trigger the two very scared conspirators into being called in for interviews by the cops and asked to explain these records. This would entail some dealings with their lawyers who would have to figure out whether it was worth their while to come clean and admit their participation in hopes of getting a reduced sentenced. Their lawyer would undoubtedly explain that the earliest to rat out the others in a conspiracy got the best deal. He who rats first, rats best.

So I had to decide on one or two courses of action: Let Chatsworth get arrested with the cocaine first and hope that he ratted out Gardner and Hollister first, and then let them be surprised when they got arrested and questioned. Or start a campaign to let them become aware that I know of the bank records and was going after them. Then, I could send a private detective to go out and talk to them, explain the consequences to their lawyer and tell them it was an excellent time to approach a prosecutor and ask for either total immunity from prosecution or at least a very reduced sentence – possibly protection. I elected the latter. I had copies of their bank records, suitably underlined, sent to Garner and Hollister by E-mail, by mail, by private messenger, all with an invitation to come speak to a certain private detective with their lawyer in hopes of making an early plea arrangement with a prosecutor. The federal sentencing guidelines were also included in the package. These were sent out three times to their home and office computers. No allegations were made. Only the bank records, the invitation to speak to the detective, and the appropriate sentencing guidelines. If that didn't scare these two rabbits, nothing would.

CHATSWORTH ARREST

Now I knew Chatsworth was going to be arrested with half a ki of coke and possibly a gun on his way between the Petronius Club and his home. Leon assured me the feds would make the arrest and interrogate Chatsworth about the bank records. The next question was did I want local law enforcement cops in on the arrest or not. This presented a few problems. First, which county cops would arrest Chatsworth? The Petronius Club was in Philadelphia County, but his home was in Chester County. His route home would take him through both counties, and might involve a dispute between the local cops and the feds as to who had jurisdiction to prosecute. Since he would be arrested after leaving the Petronius Club, the arrest would suggest that someone inside the club tipped off the cops. This tip would certainly be looked into by Chatsworth's lawyer. He would want to know who the informant was. Local narcotics cops were known to be a bit leaky with their information; the DEA not so. Clearly, we would have to exclude the local cops. So Leon/Tariq would have to set up the feds for the bust on a notification by one of Patsy's boys who saw Chatsworth leave the club with the remains of the evening's powder in his car – a late model red Audi A4.

CONTACT WITH GARDNER

By now, Ivan Gardner had received three sets of his bank records suitably underlined both on his home computer and at his office. Following the third, an attorney representing Mr. Gardner contacted the detective – Jeremy Colangelo.

"Mr. Colangelo, I represent Mr. Gardner. I am Carl deJoseph. Someone has been sending him his own records by E-mail and has told us to contact you. What is this about?"

"Are those his records?"

"They appear to be."

"I would like to meet with you and Mr. Gardner to discuss these records. Could that be arranged?"

"What is this about?"

"I think your client is well aware what this is about. He should have discussed it with you. I would like to ask him a few brief questions."

"I need to know what this is about first."

"Well, you'll have to ask him first. Otherwise, my time and your time will be wasted."

"I won't let him come see you unless you tell me what this is about."

"Alright then. Thank you for your time."

When this initial stonewall was described to me, I was not surprised. Like a bull pawing the ground before a charge, the lawyer was checking on the ring before charging the matador. But it told me a few things. First, he was not using one of the firms very experienced trial men. While they rarely handled criminal matters, they certainly knew the rules as to when to rat out and when not to. But Gardner, pusillanimous prick that he was, chose not to tell the firm about his troubles. The firm would have wanted to conduct an immediate investigation and would have wanted a full confidential admission before representing Gardner. He couldn't risk showing his bank records to the firm because they raised too many questions. So he had hired a run of the mill small time criminal lawyer to see if he could sniff things out. At least we had gotten his attention. At least, he had to be scared and was having sleepless nights. We would haunt him with a few more copies of his records and have him wonder who else was getting them. He would now be all the more concerned because his lawyer had gotten nowhere with the detective. He had seen Banquo's Ghost.

HOLLISTER WITH DETECTIVE

At least, Ms. Hollister had the courtesy to respond to my detective, Mr. Colangelo. She appeared with her attorney, Jeffrey Slifkin at the attorney's office to meet and discuss her bank statements.

The lawyer's office was a small office in a rabbit's warren of small offices strung out along one of the floors of a beat up old high rise office building at 1845 Walnut – a haven for small time attorneys. Law offices in terms of prestige are either located as close as possible to City Hall in Philadelphia or located in the group of brand new high rise office buildings from Eighteenth to Twentieth Streets along Market Street. This lawyer's office was neither. It was a building erected in the 1920s and had not changed much since. There were still pieces of equipment for operating the elevators manually that had mercifully been replaced by automatic push button panels. Ms. Hollister's lawyer, Jeffrey Slifkin, Esq. was renting a small room off the corridor of a long hallway. Mr. Colangelo was greeted by Mr. Slifkin at the front desk and escorted back to his office where Ms. Hollister was already sitting in front of Mr. Slifkin's desk. Mr. Slifkin moved the coat rack behind his desk so Mr. Colangelo could sit in the other chair facing the desk.

"What's this all about?" proffered Mr. Slifkin. An unkempt man of indeterminate age – balding, about late fifties, early sixties one would guess, in a rumpled mostly polyester brown suit, with a shirt somewhere between yellow and orange, and a bluish tie.

"Good morning, Mr. Slifkin, Ms. Hollister. I have already sent you copies of Ms. Hollister's bank statements showing large deposits over the 12 month period. All these deposits come by wire from an offshore Cayman Island bank. I'd like to ask some questions about them."

"Where did you get her statements from?"

"Franklin National Bank."

"Yes, yes, but who gave them to you? They're confidential."

"Perhaps. But it is interesting that the wire money comes from the same Cayman Island's bank as the $3.1 million were went into. The same wire Ms. Hollister claimed had been sent by Mr. Jacobson."

"But, these account documents were illegally obtained."

"Not necessarily."

"But let's get to the point, Mr. Slifkin, Ms. Hollister received $300,000 wired from the same offshore bank as the $3.1 million went into. Can she explain this let us say coincidence?"

"This is private information, sir."

"Perhaps. But look, let us say that Ms. Hollister received this money as part of a conspiracy to defraud, and a federal investigation were to put all the pieces together, she would be looking at substantial jail time. I have sent you relevant pages from the Federal Sentencing Guidelines – wire fraud, theft, use of sophisticated means, perjury, obstruction of justice, just to name a few. I'm figuring six and a half years minimum plus she would owe restitution for the full amount, $3.1 million plus a hefty fine." Ms. Hollister looked anxiously at Mr. Slifkin.

"But these documents were illegally obtained."

"Perhaps. But the feds can obtain them legally with a grand jury subpoena."

"Why are you here then?"

"As a distinguished lawyer like yourself knows well, 'he who rats first, rats best.' There is no arrest yet. She hasn't been arrested. If she comes in first and retracts her trial testimony implicating Mr. Jacobson, she could possibly get immunity and she could persuade the government to go after the other co-conspirators for the $3.1 million restitution. That's what a smart person might do to save herself."

"But she hasn't even been charged with a crime as yet. You have nothing on her. Why would she even consider that?"

"Like I said, 'she who rats first...' Don't you think the feds will put the rest of these facts together?" Mrs. Hollister was fidgeting in her seat and looking at Mr. Slifkin.

"I think Ms. Hollister wants to talk to me outside. Will you excuse us?"

"Sure." They got up and went into the hallway. After at least a half hour, they returned.

"Mr. Colangelo. We having nothing further to say."

"Then, my only question is do you trust the lawyers in this scheme not to rat you out first? I mean, you can roll over on your co-conspirators just as easily and get the benefit of early cooperation." Mr. Colangelo got up to leave.

"Hold on, Mr. Colangelo, which lawyers? Who are they?"

"Ah, Mr. Slifkin, you'll have to ask your client. Maybe these lawyers will speak first Maybe they won't want Ms. Hollister to talk at all."

"What do you mean by that?"

"Just saying."

"Saying what?"

"Good day, Mr. Slifkin, ma'am."

Talk with Lawyer
Post Colangelo

I was on the phone with my lawyer about the Colangelo efforts to speak to Ms. Hollister and Mr. Gardner. Unfortunately down the hall was a collective sing-along with the inmates providing all parts of some favorite hip hop melodies. The first was the "Funky Cold Medina" – a big favorite. With the various inmates chanting the bass rap, some dancing, and one of the jail favorites – "Little Pickle" Henry doing the dance steps.

"Hello, Mr. Hirshberg, how did Colangelo do?"

"Not bad... he..."

"The girls are all around but none of them..."

"Sorry. I can't hear. What did you..."

"My threads are fresh and I'm looking def..."

"He did speak to Ms. Hollister and..."

"Having drinks with a no-name chump..."

"Nothing."

"What she said nothing?"

Yes. She listened but didn't bite."

"Funky Cold Medina."

In between a few more of the chorus and choral accompaniments with guitar riffs, and simulated drum rhythms, I was able to get the gist of the Colangelo's report. I had to thank my lawyer profusely. I hadn't sent him any money since I had been sentenced and he was working for free and even getting Colangelo to work on spec. I told him about the possible arrest of Chatsworth. I could tell he felt a lot closer to being paid.

The prison glee club was warming up to a chorus of "Push It Real Good."

"Ooh, baby babee, Ooh baby babee!"

"Thanks for your effort, Je… I really appreciate it."

"Push it, push it real good."

We hung up. I was feeling a lot better. I definitely felt some progress. I walked over and saw the dance line of inmates in perfect unison dancing the hip hop steps. With no fear. I went to the end of the chorus line and tried to pick up the beat.

"Baby… babee!"

My presence drew howls, knee slapping and hands over eyes especially from my Old Black Guys mates.

I promised myself I would order a Funky Cold Medina my first day of freedom. The Internet says you mix equal one ounce measures of Absolut vodka, Southern Comfort peach liqueur, Blue Curacao liqueur, and a splash of cranberry juice. If could keep the first one down, I might order a second.

Funky Cold Medina.

PETRONIUS TIPOFF

Thanks to Tariq/Leon, the feds DEA had two cars poised at the entrance to the Schuylkill Expressway to pick up Chris Chatsworth's red Audi A4 as it stopped at the light at Thirty-second and Market. It was getting on past midnight. One of Patsy's men tapped the speed dial button on his phone to Agent Carlson riding shotgun in the gray Ford Focus.

"We're clearing out. He's leaving now."

"Got it."

A third car was sitting on the street as the red Audi swung out of the parking lot and over Thirty-third street south toward Market. Agent Thompson spoke, "He's onto 33, south to Market. He's got a passenger."

A second black Ford Focus parked on Market swung in behind the Audi and radioed to Carlson, "Got him, he's at the light – 32 and Market."

"Eyes on. We're good."

As the Audi turned onto Thirty-Second Street, the black Focus put lights on and hit the siren and pulled behind the Audi. The gray Focus pulled up in front as the Audi slowed.

The Audi pulled to a stop.

Carlson got out of the Focus, wearing a blue jacket with DEA on the front and held up his badge. Thompson also got out of the black Focus – also flashed his badge.

"Sir, could you please exit the vehicle?"

"What… What's this all about?" Chatsworth said through the open window.

"Please sir… Could you get out of the vehicle?"

Chatsworth got out of the car. The passenger stared out the other window as Thompson walked over to his side. The passenger raised his hands and also motioned if he should get out. Thompson said, "Yes, please sir... please get out."

Chatsworth had now been escorted to the rear of the Audi and was being patted down.

"Please sir, remain with your hands on the trunk."

By now, the passenger was also bent over the trunk and was being patted down.

Carlson now went into the driver's side door and sat in the driver's seat and began to search the console.

"Bingo." He held up a half plastic bag of white powder and handed it to his partner. He reached back into the console and using a pen from his pocket drew out a silver small automatic, looking like a .32 and handed it to his partner who slid a pen into the barrel. The partner bagged the powder and gun separately and began writing on the hood of the Audi on the white slip along the top of the bags.

Chatsworth began to whine, "But. Sir..."

Carlson began to recite the Miranda warnings to both men. Chatsworth pulled away. His eyes were bleary and he staggered back. "But... Officer." He obviously had been drinking or something. He was disheveled. So was the other passenger.

The feds called for backup. "Okay, sir, if that's what you want."

The Philadelphia Police car pulled up and the driver got out. "Officer, could you administer a field sobriety test on Mr. Chatsworth here?"

"Be glad to." As the sobriety test was administered Chatsworth was blubbering and bitching the entire time. Eventually, Chatsworth was hand cuffed and released to the Philadelphia Police for a drunk driving arrest. He would spend the night in the drunk tank and be brought up the next morning for a bail hearing. Thompson got in the police car with Chatsworth so that he could be able to file a detainer on Chatsworth. This meant he would be held in the Philadelphia prison system even after the drunk driving bail hearing on federal narcotics charges until a federal bail hearing could be heard a few days later.

The passenger, since the bag of cocaine and the gun, were in the console between them, was also held on the federal narcotics and gun charge and taken to the federal prison. He had been read his rights. It turned out that he was Henry Morgan Browning, III, an investment banker also drunk, but not driving, getting a lift home with Chatsworth since he was more intoxicated. Although he had been read his rights, he began to mumble.

"It's not my coke, and it's not my gun. They're Chris'."

"Well, tell us about the Petronius Club."

"Well, we meet and have a drink."

"Do you have women there?"

"Yeah a few dancers, sometimes."

"Do the girls have intercourse with the men?"

"Oh. I wouldn't know. Maybe. Sometimes. But not me." He was probably protecting his marriage, we weren't interested in a vice arrest.

"How about coke? Do you men do that?"

"Some do."

"Who brings it in?"

"One of the guys. I would know."

"Did Chatsworth bring it in?"

"Yeah. Sometimes, he does."

"Does he charge for it?"

"I don't know. I think the guys chip in for a bag. I don't know."

"Was that Chatsworth's bag we found?"

"Yeah… not mine."

"Did he bring it in tonight?"

"Yeah. It was his turn."

"Where did he get it?"

"I don't know, somewhere on the street."

"We need you to make a more formal statement. Can you do that?"

"I better get a lawyer."

"Okay, you said it. You can get one, but then we have to h old you on joint possession until the prosecutor will agree to drop the charges."

"Gee… I don't want to do all that."

"Well, if you ask for a lawyer, we'll have to hold you for joint possession."

MEANWHILE BACK
OF THE PRISON

I was feeling energized by the reports back from my lawyer. My accusers had all been confronted with their bank accounts showing large deposits by were from the same bank in the Caymans where the $3.1 million wire had gone from Franklin Bank. Chatsworth had been arrested by the feds with cocaine and a gun, but he hadn't confessed yet. Tariq told me he was beginning to put pressure on Hollister by a few thugs in West Philadelphia. Something could pop any minute. Meanwhile, I couldn't sit still. Jail is primarily boring. Most of the conversations are just plain dumb, the food is bland and I think has something in it to keep us calm like saltpeter or thorazine, but I can feel slow and dopey after lunch. So I have been doing thing that I can do. I make lists and I do them. I must be a bit compulsive. I don't like to relax.

So far, I have written to a number of trade schools to see if they might be interested in setting up classes in the prison. The federal government and the state combine to give a student about half his fee for a course, so if I could get the other half somehow I could get courses started – practical nursing, carpentry, automotive, heating and air conditioning, cosmetics and beauty. I went through the whole phone book. I got permission from the assistant warden to make the calls. I got three schools so far. Long distance driving along with the commercial driver's license, tailoring and shoe repair, and cooking. I got the grants checked out, then I called the schools to check out their prices and got a 25 percent reduction if I could get five men per class. I got a few bucks out of the prison's budget and a few grants from some local foundations. The men signed up fast even though it cut into their time in the yard to play basketball.

I got a few social work agencies to give us a few hours a week to administer occupational tests to see what these guys might be good at and then find them jobs.

My best effort was a halfway house. One of my old real estate clients was a developer. He and I worked on a plan to rehab a building to house 100 men in the City to have them live out the last few months of their sentence if they had a job. The prison cost $28,000 per man per year, so we got the Bureau of Prisons to agree to give us $25,000 per year or $71 per day. My ex-client said it would be a piece of cake. He knew he could buy an old industrial building and staff it for way under that number. He was working on it now and had picked out the industrial building in the heart of North Philadelphia. He was visiting other halfway houses to get an idea of their staffing, their layouts. Most of these prisoners were not violent, but had been away from the City and their families for over three and some as many as 15 years. A halfway house was a win-win for everyone. They worked, paid their room and board, the state saved the cost of a prison, my client made a nice profit and I had done something other than feeling sorry for myself.

Then at night, I could join in the rap concert and try to keep up with the steps. Tonight was "Busta Move" – I nailed it or so I thought although I had quite a few laughing critics. I think they were calling me Poindexter.

CHATSWORTH ARREST

Chris Chatsworth was first processed for a drunk driving arrest at the Philadelphia County Central Police Station. He blew into a breathalyzer which showed a .14 percentage of alcohol in his blood. More than enough for an arrest and trial. After 12 hours in the waiting cell in the basement, he was brought up and granted "ROR" bail and released on his own recognizance – i.e. he was free to go on the DUI charge until trial. The Philadelphia Police then drove him a few blocks to the Federal Detention Center where he would be held until he could have a bail hearing on his cocaine and gun arrest. By this time he had called the law firm and they sent down a trial lawyer for his bail hearing. Again, he was released on his own recognizance. And given a hearing date in 10 days to determine whether there was probable cause to hold him for trial.

By this time, the newspapers got hold of the story and had pictures of a very disheveled Christopher Chatsworth – partner in a prestigious Center City law firm – arrested for possession of cocaine and a loaded gun. Unlike me, he could be released. The court, once it heard, I had stolen $3.1 million and it was stashed in the Cayman Islands, thought I might flee. Chatsworth was married, owned a home, had children and was a partner in a law firm and was little risk to flee. He went home that day after two days in jail, and took a long nap. The next day the senior partners in the firm wanted him to come in and explain what was going on. Of course, he could refuse, but then he might be dismissed from the firm.

There were a few options: He could simply fall on his sword and admit his guilt, but then he was looking at a dismissal from the firm, and basically an end to his happy and successful life. He could deny everything, hope for the best with a jury and try to pin the drugs and gun on his passenger who had already been let go. No. The best game in federal court was to try to rat out someone else and get what the feds call a 5K1 motion. This is where you "cooperate" with the federal prosecutor and he tells the judge who then cuts your sentence way down from the recommended guidelines total. But there were several wrinkles in these plea deals. First, once you told the feds everything, you could not falsely implicate someone else or conceal someone else's complicity in the crime. Plus you had to answer truthfully all their questions or the deal was off.

So he showed up at the federal prosecutor's office with the law firm's lawyer, Charles Dixon, Esq., in tow for what is called a proffer. Basically, you tell them your story and they tell you whether they believe you. If they don't accept your story, you go to trial, but they can use your story against you if you tell a different story at trial. Of course, if you don't testify as you have the right to do, they cannot use your story against you. This is all set out in a "proffer letter" which spells out the rules.

Mr. Dixon, one of the firm's trial men and Chris Chatsworth went to Seventh and Chestnut Streets, and up the elevator to the eleventh floor. They walked into a reception area, signed in and were given badges indicating they were visitors. They sat for a few minutes before a young woman came to the reception area.

"Mr. Chatsworth, Mr. Dixon, follow me." They walked down a labyrinth of corridors all neatly painted bright blue and into a conference room where two men sat with a file box on the table. All introduced themselves and sat.

Chatsworth and Dixon were impeccably dressed in dark gray suits, white shirts and regimental striped ties. Each wore highly polished black tasseled loafers. These men were dressed for power. Dixon was in his mid-fifties, had tried cases for 30 years. He had a mane of white hair and a handsome face with a country club tan.

Okay. So the best hope, and only hope was to rat out someone else. So Chatsworth with the coke and gun in his car was clearly guilty of something serious. So, let's rat out Patsy and his friends at the Petronius Club.

Chatsworth started, "Well, you know, the coke in my car, I got it from the owner of the Petronius Club. The club is a bunch of guys who come in one or two times a week for dinner and a few laughs. Sometime ago, the owner of the club brought in some coke and a few of the guys tried it and it got to be a thing for a few of them. The night I was arrested, I was just taking what was left over home because I am the treasurer. It was just entrusted to my safe keeping, I wasn't selling it but the owner was."

The prosecutor and the DEA agent were carefully taking notes. The federal prosecutor, Hank Miller, was a young guy with a crew cut and a bad suit. He had the air of a Midwest farm boy. He was tall and broad shouldered. The DEA agent, Tom Philbin, was a middle aged black man, short and stocky, with some gray hair appearing in his crew cut. He wore a dress shirt and khakis.

Philbin looked up after completing his notes. "You say the owner bought the stuff and sold it to you for use at the club."

"Yeah."

"Did he sell it to you personally?"

"No. He put the bag on the table and the guys chipped in until he had $18,000."

"Did you chip in?"

"No. I am just a drinker."

"Who counted the money?"

"The owner."

"Didn't anyone from the club count the money?"

"No. They watched while he counted it."

About this time, another man came in the room.

"Sorry, I'm late. Mr. Chatsworth, Mr. Dixon, I'm John Harvey, FBI," he said, showing his badge.

Hank Miller continued, "So you didn't buy the coke, and you didn't help pay for it."

"Yes. That's right."

"And it only came into your possession because you were keeping it in your possession as treasurer for the next meeting?"

"That's right."

"Can you identify the owner?"

"Yes." He was then shown an array of photos including Patsy and the head waiter at the club. He picked out the head waiter, but not Patsy.

"What were you doing with the gun?"

"I have a permit. I'm legal. Sometimes my investigations take me to dangerous areas, so I carry it for my protection."

"Miller and Philbin then pulled their chairs close together and began to whisper. Finally, they looked up and said, "Will you excuse us for a minute?"

"Sure."

At this point, Harvey, the FBI man, said, "Do you mind if I ask a few questions?"

The lawyer, Tom Dixon, said, "Of course not, ask away."

Harvey then began to spread out a series of bank statements on the conference table with the bright lines drawn on a number of entries. "Aren't these your bank account records, your checking account, home equity account, and mortgage?" Clearly, they were. Uh-oh. Where was this going?

"Yes. I guess they are."

"We see some large deposits going into those accounts over the last several months. We have bright lined them. Can you see those?"

"Can I speak to my lawyer for a second? Outside?"

"Sure."

Now Harvey was left alone in the room. First, Miller and Philbin returned. Harvey showed them the bank records he had put in front of Chatsworth and explained that he had left to confer with his lawyer. Shortly thereafter, Chatsworth and Dixon returned.

Miller started, "Can we continue?" Chatsworth looked warily at his attorney, Mr. Dixon.

"I guess so."

"I'd like to show you some photos and ask you if you can tell me if you are in them." The first showed Chatsworth in his red Audi pulling up on a side street in Philadelphia talking to a tall black man in a hooded sweatshirt looking in the window of the car.

"That's my car. Yes. I guess that's me."

"These were taken the night of your arrest. Was this a drug transaction?"

"Uh. No."

"What were you doing there?"

"... asking directions."

"Why were you at 63rd and Cobbs Creek Boulevard?"

"I must have gotten lost."

"Let me show you another picture." It showed Chatsworth reaching his hand out the window to the man on the sidewalk. "What were you giving this man?"

"Uh… can I speak to my lawyer again?" They got up and left. They returned shortly.

Mr. Dixon spoke for the first time. "Gentlemen, can we discontinue this session for a bit. I need to discuss a number of things with my client."

"Mr. Dixon, we have several more pictures. I have to say that it clearly looks like Mr. Chatsworth not only bought the drugs, but sold it inside the club to the members. We do not see any transactions between the man you picked out and the club members. We would like the true story, or we might charge your client with an additional count of obstruction. We will keep the proffer letter on file, if you would like to come in again."

At this point, Mr. Harvey spoke up. "By the way, Mr. Dixon, we would also like some answers as to the source of these deposits."

Chatsworth had turned not pale, but a distinct shade of gray. He and Dixon got up and left.

Miller turned to Harvey and said, "Joe, what's this about?"

"Can't say right now. We think it might be an embezzlement."

CHATSWORTH AND DIXON AT FIRM

Chatsworth sat with his head down the ride in the taxi with Dixon to the firm's offices. When they got there, Dixon said, "Chris, I hate to say this, but we have to meet with the executive committee."

"I know, I know." They took the elevator up to the 21st floor and Chatsworth went to sit in the conference room while Dixon assembled the senior partners. They each trundled in and sat facing Chatsworth. He was their fair haired boy, a member of Philadelphia Society, married to a debutante, living on the Main Line, a member of Philadelphia Country Club, a rising your star in the law firm. He just sat there staring at his hands.

When the last senior partner came in and sat, Mr. Stantion, the Senior Partner with the capital S, spoke up. He had been a Rhodes Scholar and headed up the corporate department, he represented some of the most prestigious corporations in Philadelphia. He did not have great social skills, he was direct and blunt, but universally respected for his intellect.

"Chris, what's this all about?"

"Sir, I think I may need my own attorney." A gutsy move now defying the firm and admitting he couldn't divulge secrets to his partners.

"Sorry about that. Dixon, what happened?"

Dixon was both Chatsworth's lawyer but a high ranking member of the firm. He couldn't reveal any confidential communications between Chatsworth and him, but he was duty-bound to explain what he saw take place with the prosecutor and the federal agents.

"Mr. Stantion, I have to say Chris was found with a half kilogram of cocaine and a gun in his car. He also had a gun in the console of his car. He had a passenger. They were both on their way home from a night at the Petronius Club. He was stopped by federal agents who received a tip from a confidential informant."

"Sounds like a tight case. What did Chris say?"

"He said he was just taking the leftover cocaine home in his role as treasurer of the club. That he hadn't bought it or sold it."

"But he possessed it."

"It looks that way."

"Did he cooperate with the prosecutor?"

"Yes. He identified the club owner as the purveyor of the cocaine."

"Did that count for something?"

"They showed us pictures which they claim shows Chris buying the coke."

"How good were the pictures?"

"You can clearly make out Chris' car and Chris in the front seat talking to a black man in a hooded sweatshirt on the sidewalk."

"What does that prove?"

"The next picture shows Chris handing the man something."

"Did Chris give an explanation?"

"He said he had been lost and was asking directions."

"Did they respond?

"They wanted to know why Chris was handing him something and what it was."

"What's your take on this?"

"It looks like Chris might have been handing him money. They had more photos. They probably show what they think is a drug transaction. The photos are pretty clear. I think Chris was set up from the beginning. They can probably prove that Chris bought and later sold the cocaine and kept the leftover bag."

"How about the gun?"

"It wasn't mentioned. But under federal sentencing law, if the gun was in proximity to the drugs or the drug dealer it is a substantial enhancement to the sentence."

"So the prosecutor didn't buy Chris' story?"

"I don't believe so."

"Anything else?"

"They showed Chris some of his bank statements at Franklin National. They showed large sums being deposited over the past several months."

"What's that about?"

"I don't know. Chris ended the interview at that point."

"Chris, do you have anything to say?"

"No, sir. I'll get my own lawyer."

"You understand that we have to suspend you from the firm."

"Yes, sir."

"I would hope that you might tell us anything that might be harmful to the firm."

"Yes, sir. I understand."

"Can you parcel out your files in the meantime?"

"Yes, sir."

The partners nodded thankfully looking at each other. Okay. The drug arrest was bad, but that was one man's bad act. But the money in his account, what was that about?

HOLLISTER THREAT

It was that time that the sun was barely over the horizon making the streets of West Philadelphia look gray and grim even in the nice neat neighborhood with clean row houses and nice porches. The trees planted in the sidewalk made the walkway dark. Juanita Hollister and her nine year old niece were walking home from choir practice. Her niece stayed overnight on Thursdays so her mother could work late. Neither Ms. Hollister, nor her sister had a husband, but both had worked hard to make their way in the world. Juanita Hollister at the bank, her sister as a nurse. Their men had left long ago and her little niece had not seen her father since she was two – long before she could remember. But this was a nice neighborhood, and the women stuck together. The block was clean, the taxes were paid and the cars parked were late models.

Ms. Hollister was planning on some roast chicken – she had set the stove on before choir practice. Then, two men stepped out of the area between two porches. They had hooded sweatshirts and wore sunglasses even in the early twilight.

"Ms. Hollister, we need to speak to you."

"Who are you? What do you want?"

"Just listen. You don't get hurt if you just listen."

"What do you want? I'll scream." By now her niece was hugging her side.

"If we walk away without you listening, you won't like it."

"Okay, okay. What do you want?"

"You know the money you wired to the Caymans from the phony bank account."

"Yeah. What about it?"

"We need you to speak up. Speak up now and ask for immunity."

"Why would I do that?"

"You're looking at big time, tell now and you could get nothing."

"If I don't?"

"Don't ask."

"What do you mean?"

"Don't ask. I gotta tell you, Chatsworth's been arrested. Speak up now or he's gonna cook you. You hear?"

"Chatsworth who?'

"Don't play dumb. This isn't going away. You're in deep. The first one who comes in gets the best deal."

"If I don't."

"Do you think you can hide? Do you think you can run?"

"Is that a threat?"

"Call the FBI and speak up." She was handed a card.

"I'm telling the FBI."

"Say all you like. But speak up before Chatsworth rolls over on you." With that, the two men walked quietly down the street. Ms. Hollister was shaking, her niece was sobbing quietly.

GARDNER HEARS

Word came down the grapevine of Chatsworth's suspension. Gardner heard it, but couldn't get all the facts. He went up to the partner who supervised his work, Franklin Bryce, a tall thin man with a heavy pock-marked face with a constant sheen. He wore a fashionably cut brown suit. On him it looked like a burlap sack.

"Frank... Frank... What's this I hear?"

"Chatsworth's been arrested and the firm suspended him."

"Yes. Yes. I got that, but what was he arrested for and what did he tell the police?"

"He was arrested for drug possession and a gun."

"But not anything else."

"As far as I know, nothing else."

"But did they question him about anything else?"

"As I heard, something about deposits in his bank account."

"Oh, shit."

"What do you mean?"

"OH, shit! Oh, shit! Oh, shit!"

"I heard he refused to talk and walked out on the meeting."

"Uh-huh. He walked, huh?"

"That's what I heard."

Gardner's Call to Chatsworth

Ivan Gardner could not hold back the desire to call Chris Chatsworth. He waited until 9:30 a.m. and punched in the residential landline number from another lawyer's phone.

"Hello."

"Ms. Chatsworth, I'd like to speak to Chris."

"Who's this?"

"Tell him Ivan."

"Everyone has been calling since yesterday and he's still asleep. Give me your name and number and if he wants to talk to you, he'll call, maybe this afternoon."

"Okay, just tell him Ivan at work."

"Okay, Ivan."

HOLLISTER CALL
TO GARDNER

Juanita Hollister waited until 9:30 a.m. to call Ivan Gardner. She called from another line at Franklin National.

"Hello."

"Mr. Gardner, we need to speak."

"Who is this?"

"Juanita Hollister."

"Oh yes, Juanita. Where are you calling from?"

"Another desk, call (215) 666-1212."

"Got it." Gardner went to another office and dialed.

"Hello."

"Juanita?"

"Yes. Is this Mr. Gardner?"

"Yes. What is going on Juanita?"

"I need to speak to you and Mr. Chatsworth. What happened to him?"

"He got arrested for drug possession."

"I'm a bit concerned. What did he do with the police?"

"I don't know. I'm told he refused to talk to them."

"Can he be trusted?"

"I don't know."

"If you don't know, what am I to think?"

"Don't panic. I don't think anything will happen."

"Some detective came and showed me my bank account with the deposits."

"Yes. Me too."

"It sounds like someone knows something."

"Now, don't panic. Let's see what happens."

"Well, keep in touch. I don't want to be the one holding the bag."

"No. We'll stick together, Juanita."

Juanita's Call to Lawyer

The very next call, a second later, Juanita Hollister called her lawyer.

"Mr. Slifkin, I need to see you as soon as possible."

Mr. Slifkin had no secretary and no agenda for the day.

"Ms. Hollister, oh, yes, come over at 11:00 a.m., I'll be free then."

Ms. Hollister made quick arrangements with her manager to take a few hours leave and rushed over to the lawyer's office. She was there at 10:15 and sat in the reception area shared by the other lawyers in the suite. She had just picked an elderly copy of *People's* magazine when Jeffrey Slifkin came in and brought her back to his office.

"Mr. Slifkin, we need to do something, and fast."

"Slow down, what's this all about?"

"I didn't tell you everything before. Is this totally confidential?"

"Yes. We are bound by attorney client privilege."

"Good. Okay. I helped two lawyers steal $3.1 million from a brokerage firm."

"Oh, my God. You were in that thing with the lawyer Jacobson?"

"No… No… Not him. These two lawyers set him up and I helped them do it."

"Whoa! No kidding."

"I'm in a lot of trouble and now I'm being threatened as well."

As all lawyers do, Mr. Slifkin – although slow and incompetent – knew the best thing for a lawyer to do was listen. "Okay, tell me from the beginning what happened." He got out the ever present lawyer's notepad and started to take notes.

"I work at Franklin National as an assistant vice president. I open accounts and handle customers' banking problems. These two lawyers from the Dunstan firm came to my desk one day and wanted to open an account in their firm's name and then they wanted to take me out to lunch. Opening the account was no big deal. They were two partners from the law firm that represents our bank and I figured they knew what they were doing, so I opened the account in the firm's name. We went out to lunch at a fancy restaurant. One lawyer was Ivan Gardner, he was a tall nerdy guy who didn't say much, but I knew him pretty well because he was always opening and closing escrow accounts for real estate matters. The other guy was this handsome, nice guy who I hadn't seen much, but like all the members of the firm he was in and out of the bank. He was giving me a pitch."

'Ms. Hollister, you've been working for the bank for quite a while and we might need your help.'

'What can I do? We're always asked to make contacts and bring in business.'

'We think you can make some real money if you help us.'

'What do you want?'

'A very large check will come into the account you just opened and we want you to authorize a wire of these funds to an offshore bank.'

'I'm beginning to think this is a bit illegal.'

'Yes, a bit. We want you to say that Mr. Joseph Jacobson of the firm came in, opened the account, and told you to wire the funds into the account in the Caymans.'

'But you are the ones who opened the account and told me to wire the funds.'

'Yes. We want to set him up for this transaction and blame him. You may have to tell the police he did it all, and not us.'

'Are the funds stolen?'

'Sort of.'

'I don't like the sound of this I could lose my job and go to jail.'

'We will pay you $300,000 if you can do this. Just wire the funds and say he told you to do it and you get $300,000.'

'I'd have to think about all this. I have 15 years with the bank and I'm an assistant vice president.'

'Three hundred thousand dollars pays a lot of bills.'

'I'd have to think about it.'

'Here's my card, give me a call on my cell.'

"So, I eventually told him I'd do it. And the money came in, we forged his name on the wire authorization and the money went out. And I got $15,000 a month wired into my account.

"Mr. Jacobson got arrested. I testified he did it. He went to jail.

"Then the detective contacted me about my bank records. You know that part. Then just yesterday, two thugs came up to me while I'm walking home with my niece from choir practice and tell me to go to the feds and ask for immunity.

"I had just heard Mr. Chatsworth got arrested for drug possession. So I called Mr. Gardner to find out what was going on. He didn't know anything but sounded scared.

"So I want to get immunity and tell the feds everything."

Slifkin finished writing his notes and then pulled back from his desk and stared off into space.

"Juanita, I think you can't trust these two lawyers. They may cooperate with the police first and leave you holding the bag. Has anyone been arrested for this yet?"

"Just Mr. Jacobson."

"But this guy Chatsworth, he's only been arrested for drug possession."

"So far, yes. But he had a meeting with the federal prosecutor."

"If you are willing to tell all, and I mean all, I will try to get you immunity, but you're going to owe back the money you received."

"I haven't done anything with it. I paid off my mortgage but I put the rest in mutual funds."

"You may be liable for the full $3.1 million. But I doubt it. Between the two men, I think they will pay most of it back. But you're doing the right thing. If we don't get there first and one of the lawyers tries to make a deal, you could be left out in the cold. If you are ready to go ahead, I will call my friend who is a federal prosecutor and see if he will hook us up in this investigation. Are you ready to do this?"

"Yes. No question. I never felt right about this from the beginning."

Slifkin made the call and said he wanted to talk to the prosecutor handling the Chatsworth matter. He was put on hold and his friend came back on the line. He should contact Hank Miller and was switched to his extension.

"Hello, Hank Miller here."

"Mr. Miller, I'm Jeffrey Slifkin. I'm an attorney who represents a client who may have some information in the Christopher Chatsworth matter."

"The drug arrest."

"No, the bank matter."

"Oh, I see... the bank matter."

"When can we meet? I think my information is fairly time sensitive."

"Okay... time sensitive. Okay. Let me get a hold of the agent in charge and I'll get back to you." They exchanged phone numbers and E-mails.

It took until 3:00 p.m. to get everyone assembled. Mr. Slifkin and Juanita Hollister arrived at 2:30. Juanita was wearing her clothes out from the inside. Mr. Slifkin was still dressed in his office casual, but then so were Hank Miller and the two agents. All assembled in a small conference room.

"Mr. Slifkin, the floor is yours," said Hank Miller.

"Okay. I would like to make a lawyer's proffer to see if we can get immunity for my client." What Mr. Slifkin proposed was that he lay out what his client might say if she were offered immunity, then the government parties would all confer to see if they liked her possible testimony that much. If they did, she would get an immunity letter spelling out the deal. Her testimony would be taken down under oath and she would be required, if necessary to testify in a similar vein at trial. If she deviated enough, the deal was off and she went to trial but her statement could be used against her.

"Okay, shoot." Slifkin began his statement as told to him by Ms. Hollister. He even told about the threats she had received, but included the balance of funds she had invested and offered to return. (They were going to ask anyway.)

The Assistant U.S. Attorney looked at the two agents. When he was finished, they left the room to confer with the US Attorney for the Eastern District of Pennsylvania to get the authority to accept the immunity deal. About 6:00 p.m., all three returned with big smiles.

"Mr. Slifkin, we have a deal." At that, a stenographer came in to take down verbatim Ms. Hollister's testimony in detail. With a short break for takeout deli sandwiches, the deposition was completed by 10:00 p.m. Handshakes all around. Ms. Hollister and Mr. Slifkin left with immunity letters in their hands signed by the US Attorney. Done Deal.

Ms. Hollister had saved herself about seven years of jail time, but probably lost her job and could never work in a bank again. She also had to repay $310,000 she didn't have. But she was out clean. Done deal.

CHATSWORTH INTO CUSTODY AGAIN

Based on Ms. Hollister's testimony, the DEA and FBI sent men out to Chatsworth's house to arrest him. He was still in his pajamas when they showed up at 8:00 a.m. His wife was permitted to put some clothes and toiletries in a hastily packed and then thoroughly inspected overnight bag. His wife kept asking why he was being arrested again. She got no answer and sat down with a bewildered look. She had already not slept well for a few days and could see her life crumble before her. She would now be flooded with more phone calls. She put the telephone on vibrate and sipped her tea at the breakfast table. Life had been rough with Chris Chatsworth as a husband – he was addicted to many vices – alcohol and gambling but at least she had her dignity, her children, and a very nice social position, thank you. She was still an attractive blond in casual workout attire. What would she do now? Call her mother then a lawyer. These thoughts came after a few hours. Yes, first mother, then lawyer. The very pleasant well landscaped brick Colonial on Applegate Drive was quiet.

The Law Firm Perp Walk

The FBI could never resist a well-publicized perp walk. There were three television networks and four print media reporters assembled in the lobby on cue. Five FBI men want up the elevators to the office of Ivan Gardner. Handing paperwork to the receptionist, the five men in blue jackets with FBI on the back in bold white letters, marched down the hallway to the fourth office on the right as they had been told, past the secretary at her desk in the hallway and into Ivan Gardner's office. He stared open-mouthed as he was jerked to his feet and the Miranda warnings were intoned in his ear. He was lead out of the office past an assembled multitude, many of the secretaries, paralegals, clerks, and mailroom people had their phone out and were snapping pictures. As they neared the reception area, several of the partners were standing and asking what he had done. They were told he was to be arraigned later and would find out then.

My God. Another lawyer down. Bad press. What would the clients think? A disgrace. How could we salvage this? Call the insurance carrier. But which one? Malpractice? Liability?

Needless to say, the afternoon paper, *The Daily News*, reported in very sketchy detail. Chatsworth <u>and Gardner</u> were arrested on charges of theft, embezzlement, money laundering, wire fraud, obstruction of justice, perjury, conspiracy and a very interesting etc. These men were from the very tony Dunstan firm, who represented some of the major corporations in the City. The reporters and journalists dug deep. It wasn't long before they hooked up the case with that of Joseph Jacobson just a year and a half before. The question flew. Was Jacobson part of the conspiracy?

Were these two in on it? The law firm partners were not available for comment, calls were directed to their attorneys – another big deal law firm who also declined comment. Then the journalists attacked the Franklin National Bank people – what did they know? The money went through their accounts. Were they in on it? Who was? What had happened? Who knew? The bank also lawyered up fast. Stonewall there.

The reporters descended on Ms. Chatsworth and Ms. Gardner. Ms. Gardner had not yet heard of the arrest. She and two young children lived in a modest house in Narberth. Her husband had made partner. When the news of her husband's arrest, and the $3.1 million crime was pelted at her from all sides, she began to shake. Her neighbor came over and squeezed her by the shoulder and led her back in the house. She started to sob. The children cried. The news media staked out positions on the street. The neighbors all came out to see what the story was. Rumors flew. Someone brought out *The Daily News*. It was passed around. Murmuring started.

"He was a bit of a snot. Big fucking deal lawyer. Wouldn't join the club. He thought he was on the way up. Well, it's prison for him, buster. Let's see if the rapists in prison think you're a snob.

Daily News in Prison

I was sitting on his bed quietly reading. I could hear a stomping noise in the corridor. Big Henry was being followed by a herd of inmates, all hooting and cheering. I looked out the cell and saw Henry beaming.

"Jake, they got em. They got the motherfuckers."

"What do you mean?"

"They arrested Chatsworth and Gardner on theft and fraud. Here read the article." I read the article so the crowd simmered down to low conversation against themselves. I looked up, Reggie and Tariq were at the rear of the crowd. I started to hyperventilate, my jaw started to quiver. I looked up at Reggie and Tariq. "Thank you, thank you all, I can't tell you…" Tears were starting to form. It was hard to believe. I had accepted that I could not win and yet…

It was nearly dinnertime, so I was pulled out and down to dinner. Massive thumping on his back.

"I won't forget you guys. I know what goes on now."

More whoops. Even the biker gang members waved and saluted. The guards gave him the thumbs up. He had come back from the dead. At dinner, even the mystery meat in heavy brown gravy wasn't bad. I ordered cigarettes for all out of his commissary account. People came up to me all evening to congratulate me. It was a good day.

At lights out, at 9:00 p.m., I finally lay down to absorb all that had happened. My God! They caught the bastards. Somebody must have squealed. The bank lady. She wasn't in the article. Maybe she got immunity.

What would happen at the firm? What would the bank do? My God, I had a gigantic lawsuit. But when would I get out? I had to call my lawyer next? What would Bonnie say? What about my friends at the firm? Would I be a lawyer again? Things to ponder. I slowly drifted off to sleep.

FUTURE PLANS

On awakening, my mind became clearer. It began to focus on two things. How to get the hell out of prison as soon as possible and then how to sue everyone in sight. Focus! Focus! Okay, first call my lawyer about steps necessary to get out. Then plan my suit.

As soon as the phone was available, I called my lawyer, Joe Hirshberg. I had already spent a pretty penny in the original trial and had lost. Joe was pursuing my appeal so my conviction was not yet final but my assets were frozen. I had managed to pay him for the first trial out of some money I had stashed but had all my money tied up and under court order and it was nowhere near $3.1 million; believe me. At first, as I spoke to Joe he was a little prickly about his fee, and not getting paid for some of the time I had used up since my conviction. Admittedly, he had done a decent job on my trial but he had lost and had gotten every possible bad decision from Judge Hawley during trial. Most of the time, telephone calls are recorded coming from prison, but calls to lawyers are theoretically not supposed to be recorded. I often wondered if they – oops! – forgot to not record lawyer calls. But I had to risk convincing Joe that I was about to be freed because of the latest developments from the arrest of Chatsworth and Gardner. Somewhere there was a statement from Ms. Hollister implicating them and exonerating me. It was obvious.

Joe patiently explained the lengthy process. First, this supposed testimony from Ms. Hollister was not released yet and was in the hands only of the federal prosecutor. This prosecutor, as most trial lawyers do, would play his cards very closely to his chest until he had convictions of Chatsworth and Gardner, who would squirm until the very last minute before accepting the fact of their jail time. So I might have to wait for their trial and have all the evidence of their involvement in and my non-involvement in the whole sorry episode play out. No. The federal prosecutor would not let the state prosecutor look at the evidence until then. First, there was no guarantee that it was credible – I knew differently – until it was established fact by a jury conviction or a guilty plea. No. Joe could not file a motion until he had the evidence in hand, but no judge would set me free without a full hearing. The judge would not take the risk of setting me free and then possibly see Chatsworth and Gardner walk on their cases. Sorry it would be a long slow process.

I asked Joe what if I started a civil suit against Chatsworth and Gardner for money damages. Then I could take Ms. Hollister's deposition and get the facts out. In civil suits, you can get "discovery" before trial unlike in the criminal system where the prosecution can hold it back until trial. No. That wouldn't work because they all could plead the Fifth Amendment and keep quiet until their criminal trial was over. Another dead end.

How about bail? At least get me out until the criminal trial. Not with just rumor, I would need solid evidence.

At last, Joe decided that he would file a motion with the appellate court hearing my appeal and get them to postpone deciding until the criminal case in federal court was decided. That would prevent them from confirming the conviction of an innocent man while others were being prosecuted for the same defense. It would at least mean my assets would not be seized and sold off cheaply. It also meant Joe would have less work to do.

"So – dead end after dead end. Just sit and wait. I wasn't getting out any time soon, but at least I had knew it was in the future and then I would have one big motherfucking suit to bring, believe you me.

CIVIL SUIT THOUGHTS

I then turned to the idea of suing my tormentors. Yes, it would be possible to sue Chatsworth and Gardner, but they might have to pay back $3.1 million first which they didn't have. I could sue the law firm and the bank – after all their employees who they supervised had used their positions to set me up while they stole the money. I would need a good law firm that handled big cases like this. I could end up with a very nice piece of change.

And then it dawned on me. Almost all law firms pay referral fees to other lawyers who refer cases of this sort to them. The going rate was one-third of the fee and the fee was usually either a third or 40 percent of the recovery. My case could be worth let's say $15 million. Surely a jury would bang a big bank and a big law firm for having me go through the anguish of a trial and years out of my young life in prison, the ruination of my law career. A third of their fee would be $5 million – and the referral fee would be almost $1.7 million for a simple phone call. It was something to think about. I could get the referring lawyer to kick back most of that referral fee to someone. At the very least that someone would have to be, at least in part, to Reggie and Tariq/Leon who got me out of this mess. I would have to think about that some more.

Contact Chester County Police

I remembered that I had one chit outstanding. The Chester County detectives wanted to know what Jax told me about a certain robbery-murder. Before he was killed by members of his white biker gang, the Devil's Spawn, he had told me about his participation in the robbery of a bar where the owner was killed. He told me the story in confidence as his lawyer and the Chester County Police wanted to know what he told me. The biker gang members in prison even tried to silence me and were brutally beaten up by my friends. Now, I had a piece of useful information. Maybe I could trade this for something with the Philadelphia DA's office or the US Attorney to get me out of prison. I called the detectives. They came the next day.

Okay, Mr. Jacobson, what have you got for us? What did Jax tell you?"

"That depends. I need your help on my case." I proceeded to tell them about my arrest and conviction in the Philadelphia court system, but how the federal US attorney now had evidence that three other people committed my crime, and I should be set free or at least given bail _____.

"What can we do, we are Chester County? They don't care about us."

"How badly do you want to know who was with Jax on the robbery-murder?"

"Badly. What can we do?"

"First, you call the Philadelphia DA and then you call the US Attorney for Philadelphia and tell them you need their help. Tell them that Juanita Hollister has given an immunized statement to the US Attorney in which she has admitted that she and two other lawyers from my firm committed the embezzlement I was convicted of. That on the basis of this statement the two men were arrested on charges of committing the same crime I was accused of. The feds will not share this evidence with the Philly DA until after trial which can take months. So I have to stay in prison until then. In the meantime, the appellate court may uphold my conviction for a crime, the feds know I didn't do. You get it?"

"Yeah. We get it."

"I will send an affidavit to my lawyer to be released to you as soon as I get bail or an exonerated. The affidavit will tell you what the third man was. Get it?"

"Yeah. We get it."

"That's my deal."

The two detectives shrugged their shoulders, looked at each other. I didn't hold out much hope as they left.

At least they called the next day and said they had called both offices. Several days passed. No answer.

FURLOUGH FOR GARDNER PLEA

When I received an announcement that Ivan Gardner was about to plead guilty, I asked for and received permission for a furlough to attend this court session as an aggrieved party. The assistant warden and I were getting along well and he was usually willing to help me out. A furlough actually means an inmate can get out of prison to take care of personal matters or just plain wander around. Of course, you earn this status by being exceptionally good, non-violent, no drug issues and have a good reason not to take flight. Of course, the fact that the assistant warden had seen the newspaper stories of two lawyers having been arrested for the same crime I was in prison for was not a small amount of help.

So I took the bus into Philadelphia a few days before the guilty plea to clear up some personal matters. My condo in Center City had been rented to a nice young lady by a realtor who was collecting the rent and depositing the checks into my account. The account was programmed to pay my mortgage including taxes and insurance, so each month there was a little extra in my checking account. And while the checking account had a lien on it, I was surprised to see that my ATM and debit card still worked. So I had access to cash. When I moved out of the condo, I put the furniture in a friend's basement and parked my car near his house in the suburbs. The car did not have a lien on it, I guess because the feds thought my eight year old T-bird wasn't worth much, although it was still a chick magnet. My friend was kind enough to drive the car one day a week to keep it working. So I got some money out of the ATM, and took the train out to my car. My friend's wife let me into the basement to get out some of my clothing. So I was now set to wander around Philadelphia like a human being. I checked into a hotel downtown. I got into my jeans and sweatshirt and sneakers and just wandered, shopped, ate at a restaurant, got a massage – legitimate this time – from one of those places where little Chinese ladies make you feel like a noodle. Mainly I just walked, feeling free. There was no disinfectant smell, no urine smell. I could get whatever I wanted to eat. I could stay up as late as I wanted, buy a newspaper. The only interesting thing was that I was used to wearing a suit around town, or at least office casual. Today it was jeans and sneakers and sweatshirt I got no looks, no respect, nothing. I was just an ordinary human being that drew no second looks. In a suit, I was somebody. Or at least, the people who passed looked to see if they recognized me. I was now free and invisible. Interesting. I went back to the hotel after a nice dinner of veal parm, Caesar salad and a glass of Chianti at a mom and pop place in South Philly and went to bed early. Tomorrow was Gardner's plea hearing and I was an aggrieved victim allowed to confront him and speak. That miserable son of a bitch.

I showered the next morning in a nice clean hotel bathroom, alone and did not have to wait for the toilet, the sink or a towel. I shaved in front of a clean mirror in a warm bathroom which smelled slightly of lilac. I had forgotten this. I put on my dark blue power suit, a white shirt and a red paisley silk tie for my revenge session at 9:30 in federal court. The judge was to be Terence Falwell, a miserable old style Republican appointee from Chester County.

The federal courthouse has always been a symbol for me of some very disturbing aspects of the practice of law. As I went down to the building – a 21 story high rise at 7th and Market Streets, in Philadelphia, I was confronted with the name – James A. Byrne Courthouse. Mr. Byrne was a severely undistinguished political hack who held such jobs as mortician, county registrar for the Bureau of Vital Statistics and during world War II was safely ensconced as a US Marshal in Philadelphia, no doubt to be evacuated in the event of a Nazi invasion ahead of the women and children. He did manage to be elected 10 times as a congressman in a safely gerrymandered district until he too was gerrymandered out of existence. It is no coincidence that the William J. Green, Jr. Federal Building shares the same block as the Byrne Courthouse, because Mr. Green – an undistinguished congressman himself, was the one who beat Mr. Byrne in the newly gerrymandered district for Congress. So the entire block is a monument to two thoroughly insignificant ward politicians who managed to get themselves inscribed in history and have totems erected in their honor by a compliant Congress and an adoring electorate. One wonders if somehow the commandment against graven images is not being violated by these monuments.

I next entered the building itself and was confronted by the metal detector and its minions of politically overstaffed attendants. At least two of the entrances with metal detectors are staffed with pleasant retired police officers who wriggled into these jobs by comfortable political connections. They are polite, proficient and pass court attendees through competently. The other entrance is staffed by some private contractor who has been tasked with likewise overstaffing the other metal detector. These hirees' main job appears to be to embarrass and harass those with federal business especially those wearing suits in an effort to demonstrate how democratic the United States is and how important they are. I chose the ex-cop entrance and was smoothly admitted to the next abomination.

There are 21 floors mostly housing the offices of the federal judges. On most floors, there are only two judges each of whom has his or her own library, two law clerks, one appointment clerk – known as a courtroom deputy, a secretary and a court stenographer. The square footage dedicated to each judge could house the entire judiciary for most counties. This was a specious homage to their perceived importance. Supposedly they bargain for an equal number of appointments. However, when J. Falwell was appointed we had a Republican president and two Republican senators who refused to appoint Democratic judges. As a result, the federal court bench in Philadelphia was packed for years with suburban county Republican judges. As if that were not bad enough, suburban lawyers often do not handle matters of great complexity or ones in the federal court which is mostly in Center City Philadelphia. They have a history of handling domestic matters i.e. divorces, accident cases, and criminal matters, not civil rights, anti-trust, complex business issues. The suburban courts also have a much smaller number of judges and far fewer lawyers. So they all know each other and the judges hold great power over the lawyers because they see each other so often. In the Center City federal courts, the suburban judges often see lawyers they don't know, who are used to handling complex matters at a high level of sophistication. Frequently they are democrats, with a liberal turn of mind, and are "ethnic" i.e. Jewish, Italian or African-American – faces they are not used to seeing in court.

As a result, they develop "black robe disease" – an affliction where they enjoy berating and belittling Philadelphia lawyers whom for years they envied and despised. It would be interesting to see how Falwell dealt with Gardner – a mix of Falwell's likes and dislikes – a WASP Republican but from a big deal Center City firm. Would he play it down the middle and stay out of the prejudices or would he favor the WASP element or would he be embarrassed that one of his own could commit such a reprehensible crime.

I was there promptly at 9:30 a.m. as Gardner and his attorneys (yes, plural) walked in, and as they passed me nodded in recognition. Gardner was ashen, and nervous. He was not a trial man, was a nervous nerd anyway and now, he was being exposed as a completely greedy asshole who had made a deal to rat out his coconspirators who had previously conspired to steal and then implicate falsely an innocent man. Yes, he was a complete asshole.

The judge came in his usual 15 minutes late, and promptly began the formalities of what is called the Guilty Plea Dialogue – There are at least 45 minutes of questions asked of the defendant to see if he understands what it means to plead guilty. The right to a lawyer, the right not to plead guilty, the right to be silent in his own defense and not incriminate himself, the right to trial by jury. But then the good part. The Assistant US Attorney is asked to read out the nature of the crime and what the defendant said in admitting to all the details of the crime. The judge, just to be sure he and the defendant, understand what he is admitting to, goes over every detail of the offense and the defendant must explain in his own words what happened. Ah – sweet justice. Kafka's machine for etching the guilt in the soul of the accused could not be more indelible.

Mr. Gardner was then permitted to speak. Of course, he stuck to the script his lawyers had prepared and apologized, expressed remorse, acknowledged his guilt and groveled before the judge. Yada, yada, yada!

The judge then permitted me to speak. I described my embarrassment at being arrested in front of the entire office, the agony of the eight months before and during trial, my four months in prison. I then explained to the judge that I was still in prison because the US Attorney would not make the evidence in the matter available to me and the Philadelphia DA's office so that I could have my conviction overturned and be released. I also expressed a desire for a bail hearing – in view of the fact – that I was actually innocent – until the Philadelphia County Court could hold a hearing to hear the evidence.

The judge turned to the Assistant US Attorney and asked if this was true. He had to admit that, yes, he was concerned that the criminal defendants might learn too much about the prosecution's case before trial that they were withholding the evidence to protect their trial strategy. The judge fortunately erupted. He directed the US Attorney to cooperate with me and the Philadelphia DA in making its file available. He also directed Gardner's lawyers to cooperate in permitting their client to testify consistent with his guilty plea at the hearing now that he had abandoned his right not to incriminate himself. Ah. Sweet justice! O noble judge. A Daniel come to judgment.

I thanked the judge and returned to my seat. The judge then finished the rest of the formalities and left the courtroom. I stood and went to the elevators. Just as the down elevator dinged its arrival, Gardner and his lawyers came to the elevator lobby. As the door opened, I hesitated. Should I get on and go by myself or hold it for them. What would the ride down in the elevator be like? A disaster, a humiliation. No. I was the wronged party. He was the asshole. I held the door. They couldn't refuse my offer. They got on. Gardner had to face me from two feet away as he got on.

"Jake. I... I..."

"Ivan, don't!" One of his lawyers spoke – a tall thin woman with severely parted hair in the middle and a pasty complexion in a dark pants suit. "Sorry, Mr. Jacobson."

We rode down seven floors in silence as Gardner turned to face the front of the elevator as he must have felt my eyes boring in. A dish served cold, but sweet nonetheless.

MEETING WITH MS. HOLLISTER

I don't know what made me do this, maybe my satisfaction at confronting Gardner, but I decided to seek out Ms. Hollister. Word of her cooperation with the US Attorney was not yet public. Of course, lawyers knew that if she had not been arrested or charged in any court documents that shows the unnamed "unindicted coconspirator." But the bank, Franklin National, could not fire her yet. They had no evidence against her, just as I had no evidence of my innocence. So I went to her branch office and waited until she was free. I was a customer of the bank and she was an Assistant VP so she had to talk to me. I sat at her desk.

"Good morning, Ms. Hollister."

"Mr. Jacobson. I... I..."

"Yes, there's a lot of that going around."

"I'm sorry."

"Yes, but you're $300,000 richer, and won't go to jail. You're not that sorry."

"Yes, I know. Look, I'm a churchgoing woman, but I'd never get that kind of money. The temptation was too great." She began to cry.

"Besides, I've paid most of the money back and I'm refinancing to pay the rest back. I pray every day."

"What will happen when you have to testify?"

"I'll be fired I'm 48 so I won't get my pension or Social Security for a while. I can't work at a bank, so I'll have to find something else to do."

"What if you don't have to testify?"

"It will never become public, but I'll still have to work somewhere else. The bank's detectives are snooping around, and so are the insurance companies' investigators."

"Well, maybe you can help me."

"Anything, Mr. Jacobson, anything."

"Do you know anything else about this wire and all?"

"Well, actually I do. Not something you can use but something."

"What's that?"

"When Mr. Gardner and Mr. Chatsworth came to talk to me, there was a third man who came with them."

"What did he look like?"

"I can show you the video of them at my desk. It's not that clear."

"You have the video of your meeting?"

"Yes, we keep cameras on all transactions – at the tellers, at the customer service desks, the lobby, almost everywhere."

"Why didn't we get this for my trial?"

"The insurance company people said they wanted it. So I pulled it out of archives. We keep these CDs for a year."

"So you gave it to them before my trial and they never gave it to the Philadelphia cops or the DA's office and it showed you with these men?"

"Yes. But they didn't know what these men were doing there."

"But, these recordings show I wasn't there."

"True."

"They could have exonerated me."

"I guess so."

"Who has them now?"

"I don't know."

"Great!"

"But I burned a copy."

"You did? But why?"

"I thought I should keep some evidence just to protect myself. You know, like Monica Lewinsky."

"Ah, Monica! Wonderful. Can you keep this a secret?"

"Sure. I have all this time."

"How do you feel about Mr. Gardner?" I knew Mr. Gardner may not have told the feds about this third man. If he failed to tell them the whole story, his plea deal would go down the drain and he wouldn't get credit for being an earlier cooperator. Couldn't happen to a nicer guy.

"I could care less about him. He got me into this. I wouldn't have done it without him. He always was opening escrow accounts, but I didn't realize he was doing anything wrong until he wanted your name on the account."

"Can you burn me a copy of the CD?"

"Sure, I can do it right now."

"That would be a big help."

"Sure thing, I'll be right back."

She returned in about 15 minutes with a CD in a paper sleeve.

"Thanks, Ms. Hollister."

"I guess I owe it to you, Mr. Jacobson."

"Thanks again." I left with a very valuable piece in my hand. This would burn more than a few people.

I was beginning to enjoy this furlough business. My next stop was the real estate agent to see if the condo was okay.

Of course, my agent was in, but the lady in the office told me the account was up to date and all bills were paid. She then handed me a stack of mail that the tenant had dropped off at the office. For some reason, these had come to the address despite any forwarding notice at the post office. As usual, ninety percent of it was junk mail, but there were the legal bills from my lawyer and a couple of letters from friends and my ex-fiancée Bonny Rosenberg. The friends and Bonny had just seen the newspapers and seen that other people were arrested for the crime I had been convicted of. They were happy for me and asked me to call them when I got out.

Now, of course, friends are friends. Many I had known for a long time and appreciated their thoughts. I was alive again. But Bonny! What to do about her? She had deserted me and never believed I was not guilty. She couldn't afford to wait for me. I was not giving her the life she wanted – country club, shopping, pretty children in private schools. Was I going to call her up and yell at her? No. Zero class in that move. Get her back. No. That ship had sailed. Besides, I was beginning to think, no I thought that somehow all this had happened for reason. I had been thrown in the scorpion pit, been committed to prison and was about to rise from the dead. A little too biblical. I had been saved from myself. The mind numbing legal work in the law firm. The mind numbing existence of marriage to a country club wife. Was I feeling something? What was it? No. I just ignore Bonny. She had been a mistake of my past. What lay ahead, I did not know.

Meeting with DA

I thought I would represent myself and talk to the District Attorney from Philadelphia to see what he might need to get a hearing to reverse my conviction, and get me out of prison. I went to his office and sat without an appointment. The DA was a large black man whose office was guarded by many assistants. I was ushered into a waiting room and sat for a half hour. At last, one of the assistants, a tall thin black man in a poorly fitting four button suit and two-toned shoes, came out to say that the DA would not speak to me without my lawyer. A glitch in my furlough run of successes. I would now have to spend another $400 per hour to get my lawyer to set this up.

At the Bank

Now, Franklin National had been no friend to me during my trial, but I had only recently discovered that I could use my ATM and debit card, so I cleaned out my account except for $100 – the amount I needed to avoid fees. I then took all the money I could from my home equity account and set my account to pay the minimum off each month out of the funds from my condo rental. I put the money in another bank and got an ATM and debit card there. I now had access to about $15,000 if and when I might need it. The funds from my investment in the hospital and medical center at Cataclump were still paying down the mortgage but would give me some cash payouts I could live on if I had to. A little breathing room.

I went back to the room, and called my lawyer. I asked him what I owed and told him I could send him a couple thousand. He seemed satisfied. I then explained what had happened in federal court at Gardner's plea hearing. He was very interested to hear what the judge had to say as he agreed to call the DA and the US Attorney to set up a hearing on our new evidence. He was also surprised to hear I had gotten a furlough – these were rare. He felt very confident that the federal judge's tirade would carry great weight.

So I went to the gym whose membership had not run out, worked out, took a sauna, showered and found my old steak house in South Philadelphia. A nice steak and a beer. I was feeling human. Took in a movie and went to bed early. A good day.

My furlough would be up in a few days, but the hearing for bail was tomorrow.

GET OUT OF JAIL HEARING

My lawyer wasted no time getting a motion filed to have my conviction overturned. The U.S. attorney as per the judge's order sent him a copy of the guilty plea transcript of Ivan Gardner's guilty plea hearing in which he admitted his guilt in the $3.1 million check scheme and denied my involvement. There was no word yet from Chris Chatsworth or his plea, but the court was sent records of his arrest warrant. Ms. Hollister's affidavit was also added. The matter was at first assigned to Judge Hawley who had initially heard the case and had been so negative during the trial.

The day of my hearing approached. The law on the subject was not as simple as one might think. I mean one of the co-conspirators himself pleaded guilty to the very crime you committed and implicated the other co-conspirators, and exonerated you; but the courts do not so lightly set free those they have convicted. The evidence must not have been known at the time of the original trial and would have undoubtedly caused a different result. The matter was assigned again to Judge Hawley as he had heard the original case.

On the day of the hearing, the court was full of reporters. Not only was the original conviction of a lawyer from a prominent law firm up for consideration, but the discovery that he might be innocent, and had been set up by members of his old firm was big news. Ivan Gardner had been subpoenaed to give the same testimony he had given during his guilty plea in federal court. As we left a small conference room outside the courtroom, we could see Ivan seated in one of the rows in the courtroom. My lawyer went over to speak to him and make sure he understood what he must say.

Ivan avoided my stare, but did nod affirmatively to my attorney as they spoke. It appeared he was on board.

Judge Hawley was once again aware that he was the center of attention and like most mediocre judges used the moment to preen before the cameras and show everyone how important he was. After a long preamble speech and an arduous explanation of the law on granting post-trial relief, i.e. overturning my conviction, he asked that we call the first witness – Ivan Gardner. Ivan was not a trial lawyer and was scared. He fidgeted on the witness stand as my lawyer rearranged papers to question him with. Ivan admitted pleading guilty to the same charges as I had been convicted of, and that only he and Chatsworth were in on the meetings with Ms. Hollister. This went in very smoothly. I then asked my attorney if he would ask if anyone else was in on the scheme other than he, Chatsworth and Ms. Hollister. He denied anyone else was involved. He had already then committed perjury at my first trial, this second piece of testimony might be useful.

We then called Chris Chatsworth and asked him the same questions. Chatsworth repeatedly refused to testify and claimed his rights under the Fifth Amendment. We then called Ms. Hollister and she indicated both Gardner and Chatsworth met with her and set up the scheme. She also said a third man was with them during their meetings, but he was not in the courtroom and was not someone she knew. She described him as a nice looking man with a suntan in a gray suit with a pink shirt who said little during the conversation to set up the escrow account and then have funds wired to the Caymans. She admitted that she had been told to implicate me falsely and conceal the involvement of the other three. Of course, she was asked and admitted that she had been given immunity by the feds, but then admitted she expected to lose her job, which at 48 was a very real hardship and she further stated that she had paid back much of the money she had received.

Judge Hawley received all this testimony in a foul mood, and made a number of testy interruptions of the witnesses. This might have been written off to simply being embarrassed at having convicted an innocent man. Undoubtedly the newspaper would play this up. But it was more than that. He treated the two who supported my innocence as if they were liars, yet they had no reason to lie at the hearing – Gardner had plead guilty in federal court, and Ms. Hollister was losing her job at a very vulnerable age and would be unlikely to find similar employment. They must be seen as credible.

The judge would not rule immediately and dismissed everyone. Gardener's lawyer approached me. "You need to help us find out who pink shirt is, or we lose Ivan's plea deal."

"So basically, what you are telling me is that unless Gardner can tell the federal prosecutor who this pink shirt guy is, he may lose his plea deal, because it will look like he intentionally concealed his identity. So Gardner could serve the full seven years instead of getting a break."

"It looks that way."

"Again, why should I help that miserable bastard?"

"It gives you someone else to sue when you are exonerated: I mean you can sue Gardner, Chatsworth and the law firm, the bank lady and the bank. But if this pink shirt guy has some connection, you can sue him and his people."

"What if I think the law firm plus Franklin National are enough to sue?"

"The more the merrier."

"So what you want me to do is basically your job? You want me to find out who this pink shirt guy is and tell Gardner and you so you can clean up your plea deal and save Gardner three or four years in prison?"

"Yes. And help him with the restitution."

"Yes that too."

"Why should I spend my own good money to help Gardner and why should I tell him if I found out?"

"Good question. Why am I here at all if I have nothing to offer?"

"Quite so."

"Okay. Mr. Gardner has some information for you which he can exchange when you tell him who the pink shirt guy is."

"What kind of information?"

"The firm was involved in your trial."

"What! They helped send me to jail?"

"We think that will help your law suit against them. It will also give you a little revenge."

"Not a little. You've got me interested. What kind of information do you have?"

"Gardner attended some firm meetings. That's all I'll say for now."

"So the firm was plotting against me?"

"Let's say limiting the damage."

"Cutting off the diseased member."

"You get the picture."

"Now they have two diseased members who they are cutting off, and those members have the goods on the firm."

"Perhaps."

"Why can't you just get Mr. Pink Shirt yourself?"

"We aren't supposed to know he exists and, if it turns out we are looking for him, then our plea deal fails. If you look for him, you have a perfect right."

"I don't have the funds to do this and I'm stuck here at Graterford because Haley won't grant me bail."

"Maybe we could help."

"I'd need at least a couple thousand."

"We'll send your lawyer $5,000 anonymously for your account. He can't know where it came from. Just you. Hire a detective and get started."

"So you want me to find out pink shirt, tell you first, you update your statement to the federal prosecutor, you get credit for the information in your plea deal, you rat out what happened at the firm meetings, I get them cold. Okay. I get it. I'm in. But I want some assurance that I get the information about the firm if I do my part."

"Hmm. Good point. Who do you trust?"

"At this point, no one."

"Okay, I have an idea. I meet with your lawyer and exchange the evidence face to face in his office. You get your evidence when I get mine. Both in affidavit form. Dates, times, everything."

"Let me talk to my lawyer about this. I'll be back to you."

"Fair enough."

Meeting with Reggie and Tariq about Pink Shirt

After the meeting with Gardner's lawyer, I could feel my heart pounding. I couldn't believe I had been set up by people I knew. I mean I worked every day with Ivan, he was a jerk, but he saw me every day. How could he conspire to put me in prison? Chatsworth, I did not know. He was an entitled hail-fellow-well-met preppie. I was just a junior associate – an easy target. But now, it seemed the firm had plotted against me – cutting me off like a gangrene limb. No support. I mean I had at least saved one deal for them, but then memories are short. Maybe I was just not one of their gang – WASP-y, socially connected. Who knew? But now, Ivan's lawyer sent chills down my spine. I went to lunch with a thousand thoughts in my head. Did I want revenge? Did I want money? Hell yeah! Where to start? Let the ideas sift through my head.

Back in prison, I sat at the Old Black Guys' table as usual. We had the very festive (but also very cheap) Mexican meal of tacos and fajitas with ground beef called "carne asado." Of course the Latino prisoners were happy and put jugs of hot sauce on their trays. I have to admit it wasn't too bad, but I hardly felt like breaking into an impromptu Mexican hat dance. Not even when one of the Latinos broke out his harmonica and played "La Bamba." Perhaps this lifted my mood because I knew what I had to do next: Consult Reggie and Leon/Tariq.

They were always happy to consult with me. I had promised them part of the referral fee for my suit, and had given them lots of "White Jewish guy lawyer advice" as they called it. They came back to my "consulting office" and heard my tale of discovery bringing them up to date. I thanked them again for cracking the case – I mean the bank records were great, and the connection between the Cayman Islands bank and the account was a master stroke. I owed them big. Now the case was turning my way. After a few minutes digesting the story, Reggie and Leon looked at each other and began to laugh.

"What... what's this?"

Leon explained, "You know for an Ivy League white boy, even a Jewish one, you are a smacked ass. You just don't think like a scumbag." Reggie still laughing was slapping his thigh.

"What do you mean?"

"You know we been on the wrong side of the justice scale for years. You don't see it. We do every day. You been set up."

"How?"

"They wired the judge. It happens, especially these big guys. They do it in a very polite way, but you're still fucked."

"You mean, they called Judge Hawley and fixed my case."

"From the beginning. They got him assigned, they cut off your discovery and they got you convicted. And all the time without a jury. You were screwed, blued and tattooed."

"Okay, I can see that, man. What do I do?"

"First, we get the feds to examine their phone call records. One or two phone calls to the judge might pass, but I bet they had a bunch. I bet they took him to lunch, even golf or whatever you white guys do when you want to talk sneaky business. Phone calls. Get the phone records."

"I'll do better than that," said Reggie.

"Oh no. Another girl friend at the telephone company."

"Yup. One of my guy's Muslim wives. We are wired in. Sit back and watch Uncle Reggie in action."

"No shit."

"Yeah. Get the firm's phone number – all phone numbers from the land lines. These white guys don't do burn phones and text messages. Then get me the judge's City Hall number. I'll get the judge's home and cell. You think the bank records were good, wait till you see the telephone records."

"I can find out if they had any legitimate business with the judge by checking the computer. See if there was any reason to have a phone call."

"That's fine. But one side can't call the judge without both sides being on the line. Anything that is not a conference call is bad. Get me."

"Yeah, Reggie. I get you. That's what we call an ex parte communication. Highly irregular."

Waiting for Judge Hawley

The wait continued for Judge Hawley's findings. It was not a week. He clearly heard evidence by two people who admitted they had committed the crime, gone to the feds and were suffering major personal tragedies as a result. Yet Judge Hawley had taken no action and I was still in the slammer.

But I have to say I had grown used to the routine. Somehow, I had been meant to learn something. As my life scrambling for success in a big law firm protecting moneyed interests was receding into the distance, I was feeling a sense of freedom. Those days of pressure and working 60 and 70 hours, handing in my timesheets and billing records were a distant memory. Although I was an outsider in the prison population, I enjoyed some respect and gratitude. My weight lifting gave me a framework for my time. I looked forward to working towards new personal records. My diet was pretty good, no sweets, no alcohol, and much of our food we grew ourselves or came from local farms. I have to admit that my basketball had not improved. The guys had seen my awful looking jump shot and no longer passed me the ball. I had gotten better playing handball off the wall, but only among the Old Black Guys gang, not the kids.

But every minute, the thought lingered: What was up with Judge Hawley and where were his phone records.

PHONE RECORDS

It took about a week, but another massive legal delivery came for me.

The law firm had about 460 lines attached to its "trunk lines." This was easy to get, so I handed the list to Reggie and he somehow faxed them to someone who put them in the hands of some guy's Muslim wife. (This term means a guy's second, third or fourth wife without divorcing any of the previous ones. This is obviously, illegal, but does comply with Islam where men may have four wives.) Somehow someway, a massive box was delivered anonymously to my lawyer's office. We had all the judge's calls, and 460 call records from all the law firm's lines. This filled three big cardboard boxes and covered a period from Hawley's appointment to my case until my conviction – a period of four months. My lawyer had them FedEx'd to the prison and we started to pore through the lists. I selected out only the litigation partners in the firm – that got us down to six lines. The judge's City Hall line and home phone records were pretty thin so that cut out most of the work. We found seven phone calls during that time – most all lasting at least a half hour. Six of the phone calls were from one partner's secretarial line, not his own, that partner was the head of the litigation department. Allen Haynesworth, a man in his early 60s with a spotless record and a great reputation as a man who tried mostly commercial-business type cases. He had no criminal background. In fact, the entire firm had no commercial or even civil cases in the Philadelphia court system during that time. They had some estate cases involving wills and trusts, but no civil cases – not even an automobile accident, a divorce, or a personal injury case of any kind during those four months. There was no reason to have Haynesworth call Hawley at all. Holy shit! This was bigger than I thought.

Another Hearing in Court

The guard came by my cell at 6:30 a.m. with a message. Judge Hawley had scheduled a hearing that day at 4:30 p.m. I should be ready for a van after lunch to go back to Philadelphia. I went to breakfast and couldn't sit still. I had to think. Why didn't he just issue an order and set me free? Or at least grant me bail? But a hearing? Wouldn't there be newspaper reporters? I decided to go to court in my prison jumpsuit – a loose fitting bright orange thing and my prison issue Converse high tops without socks. If the media were there to take pictures, it might leave an indelible impression in the public's mind that I was a criminal to some, but to others it would garner sympathy. I mean I was a totally innocent man.

I boarded the van with a box lunch of baloney sandwich, an orange and a fruity drink in a paraffin container. The hour ride into town was way too long. I was escorted to the prisoner's cells on the top floor of City Hall, but brought down quickly at 2:00 p.m. to a conference room off the Judge's courtroom 653 in City Hall.

As I sat there summoned by three sheriff's deputies armed with shotguns, I was still in handcuffs. My lawyer showed and he did not seem to know what this was all about. Then some men in suits came in, I didn't know or recognize them. Finally, three of the law firm's partners came in – What the hell were they doing there? Lastly, the lawyers for Chatsworth and Gardner came in. What the hell was this?

The law firm's partners included Haynesworth – the head of litigation, Deming – the head of the municipal bond department and Gawthrop – another senior partner. Major fire power.

Haynesworth was apparently the one who assembled this meeting and spoke first.

"Jake, I can't express how badly we feel about what has happened to you. And we want to try to make things right."

"Mr. Haynesworth, who are all these men?"

"They are from the insurance carriers for the law firm and Franklin National. They will be part of a financial settlement."

"I thought this would be a hearing in front of Judge Hawley to decide my motion to be released or exonerated."

"We'll get to that when he is available. But for now, let's try to resolve this. You have been arrested, tried in public and spent five months in prison. We now understand that you may be innocent of these charges."

"I am innocent. I was set up by two lawyers in your firm and a vice president at the bank, at least two of whom have admitted their guilt and complicity."

"We are aware of that. We are aware that if this is made public, it could be detrimental to the firm. We would like to try to settle this so that it can go away quietly and you can go back to your life."

"I always like the term 'settle.' What is the offer?"

"First, we would get you a job with one of our clients at a very substantial salary under a long term contract. You would work for Meadows Community Centers – a chain of retirement villages across the East Coast – as their general counsel and vice president. The salary would be $300,000 per year adjusted for inflation and run for five years.

"You would receive $3 million in cash as well and have your sentence overturned, and be returned to normal life today."

It did not take me long to reject this, but I wanted to hear more.

"What would happen to Gardner and Chatsworth, and what about Ms. Hollister?'

"They would plead guilty and take their medicine."

"You mean Ms. Hollister, too?"

"She has immunity in federal court. But she does not have immunity in state court. She can and probably will be arrested and tried in state court for perjury against you."

"Oh, and also, you must agree to keep our settlement confidential and not to testify at anyone's sentencing."

"Does the judge know about this?"

"He's been told."

"Where is this Meadows company located?"

"Pittsburgh."

"Mr. Haynesworth, I have to say this is a ridiculous offer. I totally reject it. I can prove that employees of the law firm and Franklin National conspired to get me arrested for crimes they themselves committed. As you well know, the employers answer for the acts of their employees."

"Mr. Jacobson, I didn't know that. These employees committed intentional acts, not negligent ones, and they were done to benefit themselves not in furtherance of their duties to the employer. Our insurances do not cover intentional acts and we are not liable if the employees were not acting for their employers. Besides, you could walk out a free man today."

I wasn't ready to spring my knowledge of the telephone calls or the firm meetings on Mr. Haynesworth. Somehow that information might disappear. Gardner could go back on his deal, and the firm and Hawley could coordinate a nice excuse for their telephone calls.

"No, I understand then that the insurance carriers might not defend you or pay any claims I might bring because these acts were intentional."

Several of the suits nodded in agreement, looking at me and at Haynesworth.

"Let me understand this. If I were to sue the firm and bank, the insurance carriers would not have to pay these judgments then."

One of the suits spoke up. "No. Mr. Jacobson, intentional acts are excluded from the policies. However, to avoid litigation and in the interest of servicing good long term clients, we are making a contribution to the settlement."

"I see. So if I were to win the lawsuit, each of the partners of the law firm would be liable for the full amount of the judgment."

"If you were to win. But as I told you, the law does not hold employees liable for acts which are not in furtherance of the employer's interest. These people were on an entirely self-benefitting enterprise. The law calls it "a frolic on their own."

"So the only reason you are here is to limit the negative press and avoid a public trial. And if I agree, Judge Hawley agrees to act today on my release."

"Yes." "The law firm had no involvement in my being convicted."

"None." We'd see about that! A lie in my face, that bastard. And without any hesitation.

"I think the money is a bit thin."

"What is your counter offer?"

"I'd never thought about it. You mean the law firm's partners would pony up any more money themselves."

"Yes," Haynesworth said, looking hopefully at the suits.

"Maybe not all."

"Can I get back to you? I have to speak to a lawyer who specializes in these matters."

"But you're in jail. You could get out today."

"True, but you are talking real money. I'd have to talk to someone. I mean it's the rest of my life."

"Okay, but we would like a prompt response." The suits all got up and left the room. I was left to ponder. I learned some things. First, I could prove the firm was at least in on conspiring on my conviction if I made my deal with Gardner. Second, the firm's partners were individually liable, and might be uninsured. Third, the negative publicity was very dangerous to the firm. But mainly, Judge Hawley was definitely in the pocket of the firm and his findings were being held up as a bargaining chip. They hoped I hated prison so much I would take anything to get out. I had learned a lot. But I was also going back to prison. I was escorted out to the prison cells in City Hall to await Judge Hawley's hearing. When 4:30 came around, not surprisingly we were told Judge Hawley was "involved with other matters" and could not see us today. We would be reschedule for another time.

My lawyer sat with me at the entrance to the prison cells in City Hall. He said he was dumbfounded by Judge Hawley and would send a letter requesting another hearing. We agreed that Hawley was somehow linked to the firm and that it was highly illegal and unethical, but there was little we could do about it. We did not have the muscle to intimidate or make accusations against a sitting judge.

I mounted the van and went back to Graterford.

When I got back to my cell, I received information that Chatsworth's trial had been postponed.

Pink Shirt ID'ed

I had sent out to my lawyer a copy of the still from Ms. Hollister's CD of the transaction to set up the phony bank account under the firm's name to receive the $3.1 million wire from the brokerage firm. As Ms. Hollister had told me, the man in the pink shirt appeared to be an organizer of the scam and seemed to be instructing Gardner and Chatsworth. It had now become essential to find this guy in the pink shirt. First, it would undermine Gardner's cooperation with the federal prosecutor and induce him to exchange information with me about the law firm's involvement in my trial and conviction. Second, it would add one more defendant to my lawsuit against everyone for putting me in the slammer. The more the merrier and the bigger the pay day. Unfortunately, pink shirt was not associated with the brokerage firm that sent out the $3.1 million wire to the bogus account. We had to dig deeper and with the help of Reggie's insight, I asked my lawyer to get the detective back out to find him.

It didn't take long. The detective went to the Petronius Club and asked Patsy if he could review some of the video tapes. Patsy laughed. He knew the guy was as an old regular and founding member of the Petronius club. It was Arnold "Arnie" Mittendorf – a longtime stock broker who was a well-known man about town. He did political fund raising and had friends all over in high places. Yes. It was definitely Arnie Mittendorf. Of course, the detective agreed not to use Patsy's name as a source, and hurried back to my lawyer with the good news. As it turned out, it was even better news.

Mittendorf had been a long time client of my old law firm. I recognized the name from some of our real estate work, but I had never met him in person. A double treat – we had another co-conspirator and he was linked to my old law firm. The media would have a field day.

Hiring a Tort Lawyer

Now, I was in a position to hire a big time tort lawyer. There were several in Philadelphia, but I had to be careful to select one that would not mind and, even in fact, might even enjoy the opportunity to take down my old firm, Franklin National Bank, and now Mittendorf and maybe even his firm. I had to set this up so that I could get a referral fee kick back and I had to choose a lawyer to make the contact – would it be my own lawyer or Reggie's lawyer. Who could I trust to make the best arrangement? Although my lawyer had not been successful in my defense, he had proven a bit squeamish about continuing to work without getting paid. At least, he was a criminal defense lawyer familiar with what we call "white collar" cases – i.e. complicated business crimes. Reggie's lawyer handled big street crime – rapes, murders – and had a reputation as a grandstander. No. I would go through my own lawyer.

Next the tort law firm. The firm of Bonafine and Broberg had a good reputation in suing out big tort cases. Insurance companies respected, if not feared, them. I would start the interview process with them. I contacted my criminal lawyer, Mr. Hirshberg, and asked him to contact Bonafine and arrange for a healthy referral fee. He was fine with the idea that my old fee to him plus $100,000 would be his full compensation and the rest he would kick back to me as I directed. He said he would arrange for Bonafine to come up to prison for an interview as soon as possible.

That did not take long. A guard came to me at lunch the next day with a message that a "Mr. Broberg" – a lawyer would be seeing me the next day at visiting hours at 9:30 a.m.

Mr. Broberg

The next morning I anxiously went down to the visitors' room and found Mr. Broberg and another suited female sitting in one of the attorney's cubicles of the main visiting room. Mr. Broberg was a short stocky figure almost like a troll with small hooded beady eyes, a mop of unruly curly hair, but immaculately dressed. He wore a red and blue striped shirt with a red tie and a dark blue suit with a heavy chalk pin-stripe. Ms. O'Hara introduced as his associate, was a plumpish woman in an ill-fitting polyester gray suit; her hair was short and she had a continuously serious grimace on her face. Mr. Broberg explained that Mr. Bonafine was finishing a trial in Pittsburgh, but that he handled the business matters for the firm and Ms. O'Hara was his highly qualified assistant, and would be second chair for this matter.

I explained that I expected the conference to be covered by attorney-client privilege as I expected to reveal a good bit of secret information and I expected that if we could not reach an agreement that day would represent me that they would keep our discussions absolutely confidential. They of course agreed. I asked them to tell me what they already knew.

They, of course, were well aware of my trial and conversation which had been carefully documented in the papers and was the subject of much gossip within the legal community. They now were also aware of Gardner's plea in federal court both exonerating me and admitting his own guilt. They were also aware that Mr. Chatsworth had been arrested and was awaiting trial on the same matter as well as drug offenses. They assumed Gardner had ratted out Chatsworth to get a lower sentence. They also assumed someone had ratted out Gardner already. They figured I wanted to sue Gardner and Chatsworth, and their law firm. They expected I wished to sue Franklin National as their employee who must have been involved. They had done some initial research before coming in which suggested that I had problems: I might not be able to sue the law firm or the bank because they were intentional acts by the employees which were not designed to benefit their employers. However, they also thought that I might make a case and that the law firm and the bank had not exercised sufficient supervision over their staff and, as a result, were negligent and liable. As a result, they felt strongly that this was a good case, but with some difficulties. They would be pleased to take the matter at their usual rate of one-third of the recovery with the understanding that they would be paying a one-third referral fee to my lawyer, Mr. Hirshberg. They made this presentation in a succinct lawyerlike fashion.

"Fine. Good so far. But I have more evidence for you. Mr. Gardner has approached me through his lawyer and advised me that, in my cross-examination of him, during my motion to be released from jail in state court, Ms. Hollister had referred to a third man at a meeting at Franklin National Bank. Mr. Gardner had neglected to disclose the identity or presence of this man, and felt this would jeopardize his cooperation with the federal prosecutor. He asked me to find out whom this "man in the pink shirt" was, since he could not appear to be looking for him. His lawyer offered in exchange an affidavit detailing the contents of the firm meetings about my arrest, trial, etc. including its contacts with Judge Hawley. I assume that this will show the firm's attempt to influence Judge Hawley against me.

I further explained that I had secretly and possibly illegally gotten all the phone records of the law firm and Judge Hawley and that they showed significant contacts.

In addition, I told them that I had found the man in the pink shirt – who was Arnold Mittendorf. I also explained that Mr. Mittendorf was a client of my old firm.

Ms. O'Hara was taking notes furiously. Mr. Broberg a few – but drawing arrows at them. They finally looked up.

"Well, well, well, you've been busy. This is all very helpful."

"Now I have some questions. First, I am not sure I should exchange my knowledge of the identify of pink shirt for an affidavit from Gardner as to the firm meetings. Could we get this by taking depositions anyway? Would cooperating with Gardner jeopardize my suit against him? Should he even know I know who pink shirt is? What if he betrays me by telling the law firm as well as the feds who pink shirt is?

"I am also concerned as to how to bring out the law firm's illegal contacts with the judge during my trial and discovery motions.

"I think the timing on this is critical for my suit against the firm and the bank. So I want to make sure we agree on how to proceed.

"I also have to tell you that my old firm including their partners including Mr. Haynesworth as well as the insurance carriers met with me before a court session. They offered me a job with one of their clients in Pittsburgh and $3 million if I settled and agreed not to testify against Chatsworth or Gardner. They tried to tell me that their insurance carriers would refuse coverage because their policies did not include intentional acts by employees. They also claimed that they were not liable for the same reason. But they were offering to settle because they did not want the adverse publicity. I told them I wanted to talk to a lawyer about this."

"Interesting. It tells us a few things that we have to consider, but I believe they are concerned that their own involvement might come out – at least in your trial. For the present, I certainly would advise you to do nothing with them and refer them to us. In the meantime, we need to figure how to play the pink shirt card, and the telephone records."

"That brings me to my next point. Your fee."

"How so."

"I think this is a big case. I have also handed you virtually all the evidence. I think your fee should be 25 percent."

"I see. Well, I have to say we are very interested and it is a big case. How about if we say one-third of the first $10,000,000, 25 percent after that, and we pay all costs of investigation."

I had not expected such a prompt response, I was really testing how much they thought this case was worth. I now knew I was in the stratosphere. I agreed. We shook hands. I still had not heard Ms. O'Hara speak as they left.

I called my criminal lawyer, Mr. Hirshberg, and told him to make my files and all the evidence available to Mr. Broberg since he would be handing the tort case. I have to say he was overjoyed that he would now be collecting my fee as well as a very nice referral fee for doing very little.

Advice from Reggie on Pink Shirt

As was my usual practice, I sat by the side of the basketball court watching the game in progress. This game was among the younger guys and was a high spirited affair and, I have to say, the guys were as good as many college teams I had seen. Without coaching they seemed to know how to set up defenses and execute plays. The gunners and the ball hogs were swiftly ostracized. I also have to say that, as one with a less than mediocre jump shot, I was encouraged not to shoot and was only passed to after it was noted that I passed back. Reggie sat down next to me and asked what had been going on in my case. I bought him up to date on everything including pink shirt and the judge's refusal to even rule on my Motion. He sat staring off into the middle distance, enjoying the workings of a plot. Although Reggie left school in eleventh grade, he had developed instincts and knowledge of many things in his daily contacts with people. He seemed to have developed an uncanny ability to understand the banking system and the motivations of people in power or in charge of finances although he never had such.

"You know, white boy (his name for me when he wished to deliver a lecture of life's lessons) this pink shirt is an evil devil. I smell him behind everything. I feel he is an adversary who opposes me."

"You?"

"Yes me. I feel destined to fight him."

"How so?"

"First, he set this whole thing up and targeted you. He enlisted Chatsworth and Gardner. Now, they are caught because they were stupid about their banking – they never concealed their money. Pink shirt is playing them now. I can feel it."

"What if we look into his bank accounts and see if we can find he got the same money?"

"You won't find that. You can look, but I sense he is too shrewd. He has buried his money. See if you can find where he banks. I am sure it's not Franklin National. No. He has run his money through accounts elsewhere.

"Plus, when he is identified as the third man at the desk with Ms. Hollister, he will try to worm his way out and blame it on Chatsworth."

"But Chatsworth, Hollister and Gardner will all testify against him."

"Maybe, maybe not."

"What do you mean?"

"Okay, why did Gardner's lawyer approach you and ask to have your find pink shirt. I think he already knew who pink shirt was, but wants you to find him. Then Gardner tells the prosecutor but denies that pink shirt was involved."

"Why would he do that?"

"Okay, white boy. Lesson fifty-one. Money. Pink shirt is paying him off. He is also paying off Chatsworth so their families will have some money. I'll bet money is coming into their bank accounts from somewhere and they are paying their bills. I will check on that and see if it's true, but I'll bet we cannot trace the funds, but will see deposits going into the accounts of Chatsworth and Gardner."

"So Gardner will use you to protect his plea agreement by offering up pink shirt and will still receive his money from pink shirt, and blame you for exposing him. Neat huh!"

"Okay, I can see that, but what about Chatsworth. He's looking at over 15 years in prison if he's tried. If he gives up Mittendorf, he serves about half. He has to rat out Mittdendorf."

"Yes. I guess he does, but then he minimizes the role he played."

No. I don't buy it. Mittendorf has three people testifying against him as the kingpin in this scheme."

"Gardner and Hollister are just pawns. They only know he was at the bank when things went down, and Gardner claims he never knew Mittendorf before that. So it's Mittendorf's word against Chatsworth's, and Chatsworth is getting paid by Mittendorf. He might say they just dropped by on the way to lunch. You may have to prove Mittendorf is paying Chatsworth if you want to prove your case. You don't have access to the bank records."

"Ah. I see your point. Pink shirt makes Chatsworth out to be a liar trying to save his skin, and Gardner doesn't say a word."

"I'll have to think this through."

"Now, what about the affidavit from Gardner about the law firm's contacts with Judge Hawley."

"I don't know what it says 'til I see it. But Gardner already knows pink shirt is Mittendorf if he is receiving money, so my giving him this information is meaningless, so I might as well give it to him."

"I can see that."

Exchange of Information
with Gardner's Lawyer

I typed up an affidavit identifying Arnold Mittendorf as the guy in the pink shirt. I didn't give any details, only that he was the guy. I certainly didn't want Gardner to have any more information than was necessary. He would not learn that Ms. Hollister had given me a copy of the CD she had stolen which depicted the three men at her desk. I certainly wasn't going to tell him of the connection with the Petronius Club which showed Mittendorf. I just said pink shirt was Mittendorf. Since Gardner already knew this, but was bluffing when he said he didn't know him, I wasn't giving anything away. My lawyer dutifully exchanged my affidavit with Gardner's lawyer. Now, I could see what was in this supposedly valuable affidavit which documented the law firm's involvement with my prosecution and Judge Hawley.

As I had hoped against, but somehow expected, Gardner's affidavit did not help much. It specified the dates of the firm meetings in which the partners discussed my arrest. That was just not helpful. Of course they would discuss my trial, the information lacking of course was their discussing how to fix my trial with Judge Hawley. Of course, I had given Gardner's lawyer information they already had – the name of pink shirt as Arnie Mittendorf. Now they could plausibly deny they knew him and had to get a detective to identify him. But now the evidence of my innocence was mounting – Gardner and Hollister changed their stories under oath and in court and exonerated me. Chatsworth was clearly implicated and now we had ID'ed Mittendorf. Judge Hawley could no longer deny me bail because of the onslaught of media coverage. Hirshberg called me and faxed out the order granting me bail. I still stood convicted of the crime, but, at least, I was out. Judge Hawley would eventually have to overturn the conviction, but that was for a later time.

I got bail posted that afternoon and was released the next morning. But the evening meal was festive. Of course, the Old Black Guys table was overjoyed, but as word spread, Tariq and the Black Muslims, and the other cliques in the prison came up and patted me on the back. Even the bikers stopped by and nodded solemnly. They were aware that I had not ratted out Jax' killer or his co-conspirator in the robbery. A few of their guys who suffered some injuries in the fight, hung back but nodded to me and Big Henry.

I collected my things in a box and got a ride into town, had a huge breakfast and made arrangements to pick up my car. It was only noon, but I sat. I gave the tenant notice to vacate the condo. In the meantime, I got a long term motel suite for a month. I just sat and stared out the window. I was a free man. I turned on the laptop and got a ton of E-mails congratulating me on my release. I could not believe it, but the messages came from Bonnie Rosenberg, and some members of the law firm. Then, the phone calls from the media. I resolved to stay on message and be formal. "I was happy to be out. I had faith in the American justice system." Grudges? "Too soon to say."

I went down to the supermarket and shopped till I dropped. The fridge was soon full. But mainly I ate and let the idea of freedom wash over me.

Then Broberg called. Time to start the suit. Yes it was. I made an appointment to review their draft complaint.

CHATSWORTH TRIAL

Chris Chatsworth decided not to cooperate with the federal prosecutor and in an act of false bravado elected a jury trial so he could go down with both guns blazing. Federal court was a no-nonsense system pretty much free of political influence (except at the highest levels). Naturally, the media had been salivating for months over the prospect of some spectacular revelations to be made in the course of the trial.

It started with jury selection. Usually in street crime, the criminal defendant wanted so many of his own kind on the jury panel as possible – African-Americans want African-Americans, Hispanics their own, etc. Chatsworth's choice was as many rich Republicans as possible. In Philadelphia County, this would have been impossible – the non-white population exceeded 50 percent, but in federal court, the four surrounding suburban counties were mostly white and occasionally affluent. The problem was that the suburban political philosophy was conservative and very much law and order. Nonetheless. Chatsworth's lawyers got what they wanted, an all-white jury with a few wives of rich guys mingled in. Rich guys could get out of jury duty if they claimed business duties created a hardship and the federal judges – also usually from suburban counties – were sympathetic.

There was an interesting strategy used by the lawyers. In asking the jurors questions (called voir dire) to see what their prejudices were, the lawyers on both sides seeded their questioning with the issues of the case. Drugs, drug abuse, gun violence were obvious issues, but crimes by the wealthy and entitled somehow got in to the mix.

Despite all the buildup, the trial went through rather easily and without much dispute. The drug bust and the $3.1 million embezzlement were tried in the same trial. For some reason, Chatsworth's lawyers did not object to this and the federal prosecutor relished the chance to show Chatsworth was into drugs as well as being a clever embezzler who had little compunction setting up an innocent man for the crime. The only real issue in the drug bust part of the case was whether the federal agents who made the arrest had the probable cause necessary to make the search of the red Audi constitutional. The tip off from a reliable but unnamed confidential informant was usually adequate and uncontestable. The government did not have to reveal the name of the informant. There was little evidence at issue in that part of the trial and it was completed in less than half a day.

The embezzlement part of the case also went in smoothly. First, Ms. Hollister and then Ivan Gardner testified according to the terms of their cooperation. Although the defense was able to rant a bit about "government witnesses who made deals" it was obvious that they had each suffered substantial losses and hardship by coming forward and admitting their guilt. Chatsworth's and the witness' bank records were shone to have received substantial payments from offshore wires which came from the same bank the original $3.1 million wire from Franklin National went into.

It was interesting that Ivan Gardner testified that he did not know "pink shirt" and said he had not participated on the scheme. He did identify him by name, but _____ he appeared to be a friend of Chatsworth whom he had not met before. He said that the only reason he had remembered his name was because he used a detective to find out who he was so he could complete his cooperation with the government.

I wondered about this testimony, he might be attempting to shield pink shirt from arrest and prosecution. Now Reggie's speculation on pink shirt's payoffs was beginning to ring true.

Although the federal prosecutor took a few passes at the involvement in the law firm in my conviction, Gardner stuck by his rather bland assertion in his affidavit that the firm held a few meetings to examine what had happened, but believed at the time that it was limited to me alone in the scheme. They decided I should be prosecuted and convicted and the scandal laid to rest as soon as possible.

From what I know now, Gardner was a lying snake and I could upset his cooperation deal with the feds if I could prove he knew about pink shirt's or the law firm's involvement.

Anyway, this issue had little to do with Chatsworth, and the federal prosecutor did not get into areas which might harm his case against Chatsworth.

Chatsworth, the lying snake, tried to blame the whole thing on Gardner and pink shirt and say that he did not fully understand what they were doing. He also tried to put the coke and gun in the car on his passenger.

The federal prosecutor deftly blew up these claims on cross-examination when he asked Chatsworth – a man who was heavily in debt before – why he had been receiving such large wires from the Cayman Islands bank. He also showed how the red Audi belonged only to Chatsworth and the passenger knew nothing about the drugs or the gun.

It took the jury no more than three hours to deliberate and convict Chatsworth on all counts. The newspapers calculated his jail time would be about 15 years, and he would owe lots of money in restitution and fines which he could not afford. His wife wept copiously, but had on her finger an incriminating large diamond ring. Besides she got to keep everything that was in joint name including the house, and all the brokerage and bank accounts. An attractive woman in her late thirties with a tennis court tan and a few bucks – she was definitely marriageable.

The judge set down a day four months in the future for a formal sentencing hearing after a pre-sentence report had been prepared.

Chatsworth was done and you could stick a fork in him.

Post-Jail Meeting
with Broberg

Finally, I was out of the slammer and ready to focus on my suit against everyone in sight. As word spread of my release, I began to receive telephone calls and E-mails from people – some who had supported me, some who had not. I got a very lengthy E-mail from Bonnie – my ex-fiancée who expressed great remorse at our breakup. But, now I needed to focus on the future. My return from the dead had given me a new perspective.

Old things that were of great concern before meant nothing now. I was no longer the eager young lawyer ready to sacrifice my time, my conscience, my being for life as a corporate lawyer with no life. Now, I could only see a blank future, an empty canvas I could paint anything on. I could not regret my past, I had learned from it.

Soon, I called Mr. Broberg and arranged to set up a meeting for the massive lawsuit I was to bring. That afternoon I walked into the offices of Bonafine and Broberg PC. I took pleasure in not wearing a suit – the power symbol of the law profession – and was dressed in khakis and a sweater. The lobby of the law firm was the opposite – someone had paid a decorator something to impress the hell out of clients. An antique highly polished desk sat on a cream and blue immense oriental rug. The sofas matched and were covered in a cream and blue soft leather. The coffee tables roughly matched the design of the desk and were covered with the latest *Wall Street Journal*s and (what?) *People* magazine. Bonafine and Broberg's clients were not corporate types, but those who suffered medical malpractice, catastrophic injuries, or other highly compensated maladies.

I was ushered into a conference room and offered a plate of fruit, a soda or a coffee. The fruit was fresh and pretty good. Then the Broberg team began to assemble. Mr. Broberg, Ms. O'Hara, and a paralegal and a detective. The paralegal – Ms. Winsley was a very pretty young girl dressed n a silk blouse and an A line skirt. The detective, George Swiaki, a non-descript older guy dressed in an Eagles jacket. He was described as an ex-homicide cop.

When everyone was assembled, Mr. Broberg began, "Let's begin. Mr. Jacobson has been improperly imprisoned for the past 10 months, and was falsely convicted of the crime of embezzlement by a conspiracy of two lawyers from his former firm, and a bank vice president. You all have read the interviews, the case testimony, the affidavits of many of the witnesses. Mr. Gardner and Ms. Hollister have admitted their complicity to the federal prosecutor and testified in court. One problem: They have little money and very little insurance. I mean, a mill for each of the lawyers, nothing for the bank vice president. What does this mean? Little recovery. What do we need? Evidence that the law firm, the bank or some other party was involved. So what do we do?"

I spoke first, "Mr. Broberg, are we sure that what I say is confidential?"

"Yes, you are protected by attorney client privilege which extends to my assistants, Ms. Winsley and Mr. Swiacki."

"No. I mean really confidential. I don't want any of this other information leaking out to anyone – the media, the opposing parties, my old law firm, until we decide to use it."

"I see. Mr. Jacobson…"

"Jake."

"Okay. Jake. I can assure you that our firm and its employees are well aware that releasing any information without your consent and our concurrence is a very serious matter. What you tell us stays completely confidential."

"Okay. First, I can identify the guy in the pink shirt. Through my sources, I can tell you it was Arnold Mittendorf and I can prove he was socially very friendly with Mr. Chatsworth, and was a client of the law firm. I suspect he not only received part of the $3.1 million, but is paying it out to the wives of Gardner and Chatsworth to ensure that they do not make his part in the conspiracy known. I was approached by Mr. Gardner's attorney who offered me a deal. If I found out who the guy in the pink shirt was and would give him an affidavit, he would give me an affidavit detailing the firm meetings about my arrest and conviction which included the firm's many contacts with Judge Hawley, <u>ex parte</u>, to ensure my conviction. He needed information about pink shirt to complete his cooperation with the federal prosecutor, which he had accidentally or purposely left out of his previous statement. Since the omission jeopardized his plea deal, he needed the name or at least that is what his lawyer told me. We have exchanged these affidavits. He can now identify Mittendorf as pink shirt. I now know that Mr. Haynesworth, the firm's senior trial attorney, was in constant contact with Judge Hawley before, during and after the trial. Judge Hawley made numerous damaging rulings against me at trial which supported his finding me guilty. Anyway, Mr. Mittendorf's name has not surfaced anywhere else and he was a co-conspirator and was never arrested."

The detective, George Swiacki, started out, "That's heavy."

"Yes, it is, George. What can you do with that?"

"Well, if he is paying money either as part of the conspiracy or to buy their silence, that does a number of things. First, it voids Gardner's plea deal and puts Chatsworth in more hot water and, of course, it is good evidence against him. Plus, you say he was a client of the law firm as well?"

"Yes."

"He could be a very valuable witness for us against the firm."

"True. But, how can we prove he is paying Gardner or Chatsworth? He may be able to say he was just at the meeting at the bank and didn't know what was going on. An innocent bystander."

"If we could prove he received some of the $3.1 million from the off shore bank, and then prove he is sending it to Gardner or Chatsworth or their wives that would be a big slip."

"How do we do that? Although I had access to the bank accounts of Gardner or Chatsworth at Franklin National, Mittendorf had none there. I don't know where he keeps his accounts."

"Trash!" George Swiacki blurted out.

"Huh?"

"Trash. We look through his trash. Most people are online and throw out their bank statements. Although Mittendorf may have been careful about laundering his money otherwise, he may be throwing his financial reports out in the trash."

"Can we do that?"

Ms. O'Hara spoke up, "If he abandons it for the trash truck, it is fair game for the public to pick up and read."

"Whoa! I better start shredding my stuff."

Broberg looked at Swiacki, "George, see if you can gather his trash when he leaves it out, and let's get a whole work up of him – background, criminal contacts, family, the works."

"No sweat, Mr. B."

"Now, the second part: The law firm. How do we prove some involvement there? We now know that the firm, through Mr. Haynesworth, had numerous contacts with the judge – illegal, ex parte contacts, but what does that mean? They could have been innocent contacts, mere updates. We need proof of influence. Maybe they had other business with Judge Hawley.

"I have gotten all the firm's phone records and also those of Judge Hawley. I have cross referenced the calls and can prove the dates, frequency and the length of the calls. I can also prove that the law firm had no other matter assigned to the judge."

"Fine, but what did they say? Did it hurt you? That is the question."

"We could take the depositions of this trial partner and the judge."

"What if they deny it? People lie, you know."

"Yes, I get that."

"Could there have been a benefit, a bribe?"

"Maybe."

"Were there any witnesses to these phone calls that might help us?"

"Don't know. Probably not. Well, we have some work to do. George, let's start with Mittendorf. Then, we'll meet again."

Bonnie's Visit

I had dialed back my mood in anticipation of a long period of waiting while our suspects interpreted the information we had given them. I had gotten some takeout turkey dinner from Boston Market and was idly catching up on some of the crossword puzzles I had missed which had piled up in my suspended mail collection. Linda Ronstadt crooned peacefully and sadly in the background. It was a time to be at peace. Then, I heard the tumbler in my lock click and the door opened revealing Bonnie Rosenberg all in white at the entrance.

"Bonnie... I... I..." Obviously a loss for words, I stood up from my chair. She came over and pushed me back in the chair.

"Don't say a word." She reached for a string on the back of her outfit. "I always wanted to do this."

"But, Bonnie... It..."

"Hush," she was naked with a big smile. "I owe you." She sat on my lap and leaned against me. I felt a stir. Damn! I was being betrayed. The long state-imposed neglect of my nether region was no longer. It was astir, need I say more. We rolled onto my thick oriental rug as I grappled with my gym shorts. As we progressed, my anger and frustration at Bonnie's earlier defection from Camp Jacobson returned. It did not dent my desire, but fueled something in adrenalin or testosterone. I was more violent than I had ever been with Bonnie and she was shouting something which I guessed was a mixture of sacred and profane. I hoped we were not disturbing Ms. Johnson, my elderly next door neighbor, but I figured she might be happy that after all this time I was getting some action. After a number of forays, Bonnie limped into the bathroom and then tumbled into my bed. I had watched this bathed in sweat and started to speak...

"Bonnie... it's..." No answer, some heavy breathing from an inert form. I still lay on my back on my oriental. Thoughts of all sorts swirled. Bonnie had not gotten the hint that I was not welcoming her back into my life. I had changed. To be frank, I now viewed her as irrelevant. I was no longer the respectable young lawyer with a nice future, who needed a country club wife and a soccer mom as a partner. I was not going back to those days. I had learned something. I had seen the bad side of that life as two of my colleagues sold me down the river without a second thought.

But Bonnie. What was I feeling? Men seem to pick women for a lot of different reasons. Women pick men to fit into the life they chose for themselves. They are social animals and hold society together and pick mates for security. I was not that person any longer. But the new sex. What was that? I was not inexperienced with women, but had treated Bonnie with affection and respect. This new sex thing was never part of our love making and she loved it. I have to admit I did too. But I did not want that from my wife. Somewhere I had grown up. When I was a lad, I pursued women as a lad; lust, quick action, no commitments, maybe some alcohol. The women were to be a bit crazy, adolescent, irresponsible. Then I saw through a glass darkly. When I became a man, something in my brain switched. I wanted a life partner, someone I could depend on. I would treat her with affection and respect. I had switched back again, I did not want a wife, a respectable existence. Bonnie had turned, at least for me, into the irresponsible unreliable type, but the sex was now great. I was going through some life passage. The tunnel was dark, and I didn't know where it was going. But Bonnie was not on the passenger list. I had to tell her in the morning. She snored lightly unaware tomorrow would be painful.

Post Bonnie

As I drifted off to sleep, I realized I had made a mistake in the selection of a mate. I had allowed my community to dictate to me what I should expect for the balance of my life. Bonnie was a fixture of the community of semi-affluent professionals. She was designed to be a mother and wife in the suburbs, fully protected and secure. Somehow, I had been convinced that this is what I wanted. I cannot fault Bonnie. She had been bred for this role. When she came to my door, she was fighting for the security of herself and her unborn children in the best way she knew. At the same time, she had deserted me when I could not fulfill that role. I began to see that she had not fallen in love with me, but my unborn children and her security. I could not blame her, but I had now changed. It was as if I had been unchained from the wall of the Plato's Cave and had seen life not by some reflection but real and as part of a larger picture. Bonnie made female snores next to me, as if to say what might have been. Somehow, an unknown force had liberated me. Somewhat painfully, I had passed through some new birth canal. It would be painful and almost impossible to confront Bonnie tomorrow morning, but I was not her man.

SWIACKI'S FINDINGS

I was again brought in to see Mr. Broberg et. al. to hear Mr. Swiacki's finding. After a short time, I was ushered into the conference room – replete with water, coffee, sodas and a fruit platter (the fruit was still excellent). In front of each chair for the meeting was a file – each in different colors – mine was orange. When all were assembled, I began to leave through the pages inside the file as Mr. Broberg directed our attention to Mr. Swiacki.

"George. What have you got for us?"

"First, the trash. We found discarded documents in the recyclable trash on three successive Tuesdays – the day for the Mittendorf's trash pickup at their residence. On one day, we found discarded checking accounts monthly statements for a Sunquest Corp. which showed a monthly deposit of $60,000 and two checks issued to two corporations in the amount of $10,000 each."

"Bingo."

"Yes. With Ms. Winsley, we traced the two corporations. One is owned by Ms. Chatsworth, one by Ms. Gardner. The Sunquest Corp. was owned by Arnie Mittendorf."

"Whoa! A very valuable link."

"Yeah. The $60,000 came by way of the same Cayman Islands bank as where the $3.1 million went."

"How did you find out who the two $10,000 checks were made out to?"

"Don't ask!"

"I had to ask, "Okay. So now we have not only Arnie, both also the two wives in criminal activity – money laundering, obstruction of justice, conspiracy. Great move. What do we do now? Take depositions, get them arrested."

"Whoa. Hold your horses! Now that we know things, we don't want to let people know. They might take over. Let's see where this takes us. Don't forget, the Chatsworth's and Gardner's wives probably don't have much money. We need a deep pocket. But now we have three sources of information. We have to play them. Now George, tell us about Arnie."

"Arnold was a two sport athlete at Somerton College near Harrisburg. He was a track star and a decent receiver on a pretty good Division III football team for three years. He was a tall handsome guy who had a number of political internships with the state legislature in Harrisburg. He met Amy Kaiser – of the oil money Kaiser's – at a Philadelphia debutante ball and stuck like glue to her until their marriage four years later. They live in a large comfortable house in Devon – about a block away from Chatsworth. He belongs to the same country club as Chatsworth where they both play tennis and squash at a very high level. Arnie won the club championship in squash four years ago.

Arnie is very involved in Republican politics in Pennsylvania and is a major fund raiser with many contacts. He has contacts throughout the state and can deliver. He is suspected of getting business for Philadelphia law firms in the municipal bond business."

"Whoa!" I inadvertently expelled.

"Yes. A good point. He is very good at spending his wife's money and is very sensitive about being referred to as Mr. Kaiser. He does work as a stock broker, but earns a middle level income. As you told us before, he has used your old firm as his legal representative in the past – a few minor matters."

"Does he belong to the Petronius Club?"

"I wouldn't know that. Their membership is confidential."

"Who does his taxes?"

"A paralegal at your old firm."

"Very good stuff. Mr. Broberg, what do you suggest we do next?"

"Squeeze the wives, then squeeze Mittendorf. They are all exposed and we have dirt on them. Maybe they'll turn on someone. Remember, we need deep pockets – the firm or the bank. That takes us from low seven figures to high eight figures."

"High eight."

"Yes. High eight. But don't go out and spend it just yet."

After going over a few more details, we got up to go. On my way out, Ms. Winsley took off her horn-rimmed glasses, gave me a dazzling smile. "Looking good, Mr. High Eight."

Why did this put a bounce in my step? Focus, Jake. Focus. I gave George a pat on the back. "Thanks, Mr. Swiacki."

"Everyone calls me Swacks."

"Okay, Swacks, it is."

SWACKS REPORT
FOR THE WIVES

Swacks called me on my cell to update me on his interview with the wives of Gardner and Chatsworth two days later. He described Gardner's house as a twin in Narberth, a nice but not ritzy area in the suburbs. Ms. Gardner had met Ivan during their undergraduate days at Penn State, but both came from nearby former coal mining towns near Scranton. She was a biology major, he an engineer, both nerds. They had two children aged four and six and she had not yet returned to work with a pharmaceutical company. Swacks had greeted her one morning after the kids had left for school. He told her he was a private detective and wanted to talk to her. She started to shake and said she had already been asked many times about her husband's criminal activity and could add no more. Swacks told her he didn't want to ask anything just show her some papers and ask her to call the lawyer. He then produced the bank account records for the account into which the $10,000 per month was deposited from Mittendorf's corporation. He then explained that this money could get her a prison term and kill her husband's plea deal. Her face lost all its color and stared to quiver. She eventually vomited politely in the bathroom. Swacks told her to contact him if she or Ivan had any more to say. He left her but placed the envelope with the bank accounts on the coffee table.

He then went to Ms. Chatsworth's house – a very nice in the elite suburb of Devon. It was midafternoon and Ms. Chatsworth was expecting the children home from school. She was wearing an attractive tennis outfit with pleated skirt, her hair was dyed fashionably with blond streaks and she was wearing ample gold jewelry. She had been a debutante in Philadelphia and he met her husband at a pool party when they were in their 20s. She had never worked, but her family was, while not rich, well off. Swacks showed her the bank account from her corporation and explained that she had been receiving $10,000 per month from Mittendorf's corporation to keep her husband quiet. She started to get angry and asked if "we" hadn't done enough already. He explained that he was "we" and that he represented Mr. Jacobson to whom her husband had done plenty. He told her to contact her lawyer because he wanted to get more information. He explained that the receipt of the $10,000 implicated her both financially and criminally, and that he wanted more information from her husband. He left his card, and the bank records, and left with her cursing him as he drove off.

Swacks then picked me up and we both went to see Arnie Mittendorf. I wouldn't miss this for anything. We were invited to sit in the brokerage firm's reception area which was, the best way to call it, "corporate." White sofas, a white coffee table and a chrome and glass desk. Arnie came out. He had a small cubicle in a large office facing a TV screen on which financial information flowed. He didn't recognize me. Swacks introduced himself as Mr. Jacobson's private detective. Mr. Mittendorf started to say he didn't know of a Mr. Jacobson. Swacks waived away his protests. He carefully placed bank records in front of him and then a still of him sitting with Chatsworth and Gardner in front of Ms. Hollister. Swacks told him that he should contact his lawyer, that he was looking at a minimum of 10 years federal time and was further implicating the wives in his payoff of $10,000 per month.

Arnie was playing it cool. "This doesn't mean anything"

Swacks said, "Look Mr. Mittendorf, Mr. Jacobson here is not playing games. You are looking at serious prison time, and huge financial suits. We want information and we want it quick. Call your lawyer and call us back. It would do well for you to cooperate with us." Again, Swacks left the records and the photos on Arnie's desk. He continued to shout as we left.

"I had nothing to do with this."

Swacks had deftly and professionally set a flame under the pot and would wait for it to boil. Who would call first? What machinations would go on among the three? What deals would be made? It was a time to be patient.

Ms. Chatsworth and Her Attorney Appear

The first of our candidates for more information appeared. Ms. Chatsworth and her lawyer appeared. Her lawyer John Heimerding, was an estate lawyer who really represented her parents, but he dutifully showed. As they sat at the Bonafine and Broberg conference room (the fruit plate was nowhere in sight) they were a bit nervous. Ms. Chatsworth was looking angry and defiant, so we knew what to expect from Mr. Heimerding. Bupkas! Squat! He explained that she had nothing to do with her husband's fiasco, did not have any interest in cooperating even she did know something, and was divorcing her husband. She had evidently been advised that people might be scrapping over marital assets – the government for restitution, me for damages and the insurance company who had paid out for the loss – actually three insurance companies - Franklin National's, the brokerage firm, and the law firm had made some arrangement to share the loss and cooperate in funding the $3.1 million. It also made sense that she was protecting her children. I mean husband would be gone at least 15 years and she needed a new one while she still had looks.

Mr. Broberg quietly slid the corporate bank account monthly statement across the table.

"What are you going to do about the $10,000 per month you have received from Arnold Mittendorf?" Heimerding leaned over to whisper to Ms. Chatsworth.

"We don't know anything about that."

"You've lived on the money."

"She thought it was something her husband had set up for her."

"Uh-huh, I see. Well, the federal government may see it differently. Why would Mr. Mittendorf be paying a corporation set up for your benefit which had no other function?"

"We don't know."

"Do you know Mr. Mittendorf?"

"No." We could disprove that.

"Okay, then. You may find yourself named as an accessory by the federal government."

"We don't think so." With that they got up and left with Ms. Chatsworth muttering something about Jew lawyers. She would get no extra gruel where she was going.

BROBERG AND THE AUSA

Now armed with some of our own discoveries, Mr. Broberg had requested a conference with the Assistant US Attorney now handling the prosecution against Ivan Gardner and Chris Chatsworth. We now knew that Arnold Mittendorf had been the "pink shirt" and that he was paying through a maze of corporations, the wives were being paid, presumably to continue to conceal Mittendorf's involvement. We also knew that the law firm had a number of contacts with Judge Hawley before, during and after my trial and had been involved with him on my Petition for Release.

After passing through metal detectors and sitting politely in the US Attorney's lobby for a half hour, we were escorted back to a conference room at the end of a series of hallways. We sat at the conference table and saw Hank Miller and his assistant carrying in stacks of boxes of files. Mr. Miller and his assistant sat across from us and explained that he was waiting for several more people, and he began to dig files out of the boxes to stack in front of him.

Three more people came in. The first introduced was Amy Lodenberg, the chief of the Fraud Department, next were two agents one from the FBI, Joe Altimori, a well-dressed guy in a blazer and an open neck button down shirt, and Jim Ostreich, an older man in a gray suit.

"We became aware of Mr. Mittendorf through CDs from the hidden cameras at Franklin National. It seems these CDs had been, shall we say, buried during your criminal trial, but show two things, 1) you were not in or near the bank on the days in question and 2) Gardner, Chatsworth and Mittendorf were shown going in and out of the bank together on those dates and times. I should add that the bank and their insurance carrier had been advised to keep these CDs from you during your trial. Enough said about that. Significantly, the CD of the camera from Ms. Hollister's desk is still missing. We presume you have it. May we have a copy as soon as possible? You have been using copies of a still from a meeting at her desk, which we need."

"Of course, of course."

"We have also with Patsy's somewhat reluctant help, been given access to the Petronius Club's tapes. Enough said on that."

"Also, Mr. Jacobson, we have been tapping Judge Hawley's phone for some time now on other matters. It happens that we have known of your firm's and particularly Mr. Haynesworth's involvement in influencing the judge during and after the trial. Enough said about that.

"Since your identification of Mr. Mittendorf, the F.B.I. has been able to trace his bank accounts and his disbursals through dummy corporations to Gardner's and Chatsworth's wives.

"This of course is all confidential at this point."

"But… But… you knew all along I was innocent."

"Not exactly. We had to let this play out to be sure we shut down the whole operation including the firm, the bank Mittendorf and the wives."

"But I was convicted and spent time in prison."

"We are happy to report you were a model prisoner."

"But… But."

"We will be conducting a grand jury soon to bring everyone in and assemble a massive criminal trial against everyone."

"Mr. Jacobson, we apologize for our letting you languish in prison all this time, but we needed to build a solid case. We are happy you are now free. We hope you and Mr. Broberg will respect our need to continue the investigation without your interference. We commend you on your progress so far. We see that you have a substantial lawsuit in the making, but we ask you to be patient while we proceed. You will see very useful evidence revealed as our investigation proceeds."

Broberg, O'Hara and I sat back open-mouthed as Amy Lodenberg dryly and methodically laid out her information. We were stunned. It was as if the missing pieces of the puzzle had been put on the table. We now would have solid evidence against Judge Hawley, Mr. Haynesworth, the law firm, Franklin National and its insurance company. Big targets, big bucks, deep pockets and their teats were in the ringer. We just had to sit back and wait to reel in the big fish. Months of anguish, months of despair, washed away. Just sit back and don't rock the boat.

We shook hands with everyone and, with little comment, made our way out of the US Attorney's labyrinth of offices. We didn't speak until we were in the elevator.

I guess it was me who spoke first, "Holy shit, holy shit, holy shit!"

"Well said, "From Ms. O'Hara.

Broberg just beamed.

GRAND JURY

The federal grand jury process is a strange bird. Like other juries people are selected to serve and render decisions. There are 23 selected to serve for a year or more, but they only sit one day each week, and they don't have to attend each session. The witnesses are called to testify on all questions asked by the prosecutor, but the witnesses are not allowed to have a lawyer present. Lawyers usually wait in the corridor outside the grand jury room and hope their clients didn't screw up too badly. Only the witness and the prosecutor are before the jury panel, and no one can object to the prosecutor's questions, no matter how unfair or irrelevant. There is no judge present to maintain order. Then, the jurors are asked whether certain people should be indicted – which means formally charged with a crime. This is in effect to insulate the prosecutor from any lawsuits or public protest because the "grand jury" issued the finding, not the prosecutor. However, with all that power, no defense lawyers, no judge, unlimited questioning power, 23 gullible citizens who only attend occasionally, it is said that the prosecutor could indict a ham sandwich.

All proceedings in front of the grand jury are supposed to be secret. However, the media is always interested in who shows up and how they look before and after the session. To the public, it is a bit like having mice in your house. You can hear them scuttering behind the walls, know they're up to no good, but never actually see them. When some poison is eventually administered, there is a dreadful smell which emanates from the dead mice, but no actual bodies.

Somehow, the grand jury proceedings result in a treasure trove of guilty pleas and information for the prosecutor and it did so in this case.

Even Gardner, who was now confronted with losing his plea deal, and his wife, who now might be indicted for taking money from Mittendorf to keep quiet, were distraught and crying. Chatsworth took the fifth, afraid to say a word and was now looking at a disastrous sentencing. Mittendorf came in very cocky and tried to blame Gardner and Chatsworth for the whole affair, but was indicted because of the obvious receipt of funds in his bank accounts and his payments to the wives. Now, we get to the good part. Judge Hawley and Haynesworth did the full mafia perp walk, covering their heads with their suit jackets while taking the fifth.

As it turned out, Haynesworth, the good solider, fell on his word and took the blame for the entire matter with Judge Hawley, and made a deal to plead guilty to one count of obstruction of justice, so long as no one else from the firm was implicated. He shouldered the full blame and let his partners go unindicted. Hawley, it is reported, cried through the entire grand jury questioning and admitted his guilt.

Since Hawley was being investigated in a number of other matters, he elected to plead guilty and cooperate with the government. He was permitted to resign his judgeship and his bar membership to preserve his handsome judicial pension, and he would testify against at least a dozen lawyers and their clients. It was significant that he actually received very little money. He got lots of golf vacations at super deluxe resorts, a nearly free golf membership at a prestigious golf club, a paid membership and open tab at the elite dining club, and, it is rumored, a few visits from women of ill repute. Part of the rumor that they arrived at his chambers in black robes with thank you notes taped strategically to their abdomens.

The insurance carriers trotted out a few executives to plead guilty to hiding the CDs of the bank cameras. All received probation, but were given healthy raises from the insurance carriers.

The only ones to be tried were to be Mittendorf and Chatsworth, who would be tried together and, hopefully, blame each other. Gardner would be a prime witness against both, as would their own financial records. Ms. Chatsworth was finally persuaded to testify about her conversations with Arnold Mittendorf and got off lightly. Ms. Gardner had to surrender her money, but was never tried.

Over the months of the grand jury, I sat and mused how all these people got into such trouble over me. But the criminal case was yet to be fully revealed in public and would take at least a year before it came to trial. After waiting patiently, Broberg sent a draft of a complaint out to all parties and said he would file it if we couldn't come to terms. Once again, a meeting was scheduled in the Franklin National's elite conference room. I was looking forward to those miniature danishes.

Grand Jury Period – Insurance Company Officer

As the days progressed, I had no job, and not much to do. I had some money to live on, but major prospects from the lawsuit, but I was in a limbo period. I surfed the web, read lots of books and started to get a résumé together for God knows what.

Slowly, bits and pieces of the federal grand jury began to leak out. I heard who had been called as a witness and who their lawyer was. They called so many people – each heavily lawyered up – that I was sure that the town was running out of criminal defense lawyers. Occasionally, I would get calls from people, but I let the answering device on the phone pick up the calls. Ivan called to say he was sorry again. He must have lost his plea deal because he had not told the feds in his first few attempts everything he knew about Mittendorf and the wifely payoffs. Ms. Chatsworth called to curse me out choosing a few of the popular terms implying I had improper relations with my mother, and served a subservient role in gay male sex – both of which terms rhymed. The partners at my old law firm wanted me to come in for "a talk."

Broberg called to say the insurance carriers wanted to meet with us. They apparently had learned that the law firm and the bank were more involved than they had been lead to believe. So we agreed to meet.

Broberg, Ms. O'Hara – notepad at the ready – and I went to the very sumptuous conference room at Franklin National at 9:30 on fine morning. Not only were there fruit trays but selections of miniature danishes. There was no espresso – alas! No wait. The time was not now to be cocky. It wasn't over. The minions from the insurance carriers trundled in, they had apparently met earlier.

James O'Day, the Senior Vice President of the law firm's carrier, introduced everyone to us and began a presentation. It was laughable. He had artfully, or someone had artfully, reconstructed the facts. By now, we knew this was bullshit. We got no Mittendorf, no monthly payments, no withheld CDs, no Haynesworth-Hawley telephone conversations. Pure pap!

When he finished, Mr. Broberg pushed back his chair, drawing Ms. O'Hara and I with him. "Gentlemen, thank you for your efforts, but this is a waste of time. You are shuffling chairs on the Titanic." Nice move, Mr. Broberg, I didn't think he had any balls. As we slowly rose, Mr. O'Day tried, "Wait, wait, let's talk."

Mr. Broberg turned and said, "Look, Jim, I started out in practice dealing with low balling Allstate claims adjustors. I want to try this case. Bonafine will eat your lunch. Don't low ball us again or sell us the old Allstate malarkey."

"Okay, okay, Mr. Broberg." Apparently he had no first name. "Let's talk facts."

"Okay. First, we believe Judge Hawley and Mr. Haynesworth will be disbarred and possibly charged criminally with obstruction of justice. Mittendorf, it will turn out, was a client of the law firm, and will go down as the king pin. Chatsworth's and Gardner's wives may be indicted. The bank and its officers may be indicted for burying the CDs on the advice of the law firm. Your people have screwed up royally and you'll have to pay for it. Big time. What are your policy limits and you better show us the declaration page of the policy before we believe you."

"The limit for the law firm is $50 mill and same for the bank."

"Throw that in, and we'll go after the others separately."

"No way. A hundred mill. No way."

"Yes, way."

"Okay, okay, we'll go $25 mill for a total global release of everyone, wives, lawyers, bank employees, the works."

"See you I court." Jim did not stop up this time. We left. I took a few danishes and nodded. We walked the half block back to Broberg's office and went into the small conference room.

"Okay, Jake. What do you want? Do you want a trial, do you want money, revenge, what? We got their attention. We can always get more money."

"I'm not sure. Money is nice. I have to think over the part about revenge and a trial."

"Clearly, they don't want the publicity. It will destroy the law firm. They'll pay for an early settlement."

"Let me think about it."

Fine, we have time. As the grand jury proceeds, our case gets better and better."

"Fine, I'll call you." I went down to the street and went for a long walk. What did I really want?

SETTLEMENT CONFERENCE

One of the things you learn as a lawyer, and frequently tell clients is that a settlement is best. While you don't get as much money sometimes, you eliminate risk and, best of all, you don't have to wait forever. So when Broberg asked me what I wanted, I knew we should settle. He estimated a possible jury verdict at $100 million but said with appeals and all, I might have to wait three or even seven or eight years. I was carefully mulling this over, when we received an invite to sit down with my old law firm. On the principle that a good lawyer always listens, we were ready to listen.

I have to admit getting the shivers as we rode up the elevator to my old firm and were ushered into the large conference room where all, and I mean <u>all</u>, partners were assembled.

Broberg, the efficient Ms. O'Hara and I sat at one end of the table. Alexander von Thiel, the refined gentle head of the Estates Department, got up to speak. Mr. von Thiel was similar to estates lawyers everywhere – well-connected to old money, refined, diplomatic, non-threatening. He was used to holding bewildered old ladies' hands as they worried about their money and their children. He patiently did and re-did their wills as they sought out human contact. He was a man chosen to address me with an apology.

And apologize he did. Profusely. A little late. But still an apology. Then he got to the real message wrapped in a silken napkin, scented with the aroma of Arabia. My lawsuit might destroy the law firm. The publicity would scare aware corporate clients, political allies, and make the firm's every act seem to be a nefarious conspiracy. He recited the origins of the firm, its stability in terms of crises, the many lives dependent on the firm.

He even credited Haynesworth with bravery in taking the blame criminally for the whole firm. He hinted at hiring me back. Something was fuming inside me. I kept telling myself be cool, act like a professional. I knew I would not go back to the law firm grind and had no need of these people – the ones who silently watched my perp walk out of the office in the custody of police for a crime I knew nothing about. No one had called or offered to help. I was a contagious pariah, a leper to be avoided at all costs. But somewhere brewing in me was a rationality, a desire to do the right thing as von Thiel's honeyed words drifted over me.

I interrupted, "Mr. Thiel. Does the firm have a pro bono program?" (This is a program where the firm permits lawyers to represent causes that may be charitable or politically beneficial)

"Oh, yes."

"Do you keep track of the hours?"

"Oh, yes. We can make them available. Confidential, of course."

"How about ethics? Do you train your people in ethics?"

"Of course, we always meet our Continuing Legal Education requirement."

"So, six hours a year per lawyer. No internal program?"

"I'd have to say no."

"What do you charge your charitable clients?"

"Of course, they get a 20 percent discount."

"So when you bill $500 per hour, they are only billed $400?"

"Yes. Quite so"

"Do you have a diversity hiring program?"

"Not as such. But you must understand, some clients like more of their own kind to represent them."

"Uh- huh. Are your partners and associates required to give to certain political candidates?"

"No, of course not. That would be illegal."

"Do you have meetings where certain candidates are, shall we say, recommended?"

"Of course. It makes for good business."

"Are the contributions by members of the firm checked?"

"Not as such. It's all voluntary."

"And this list is shown to the candidate?"

"Of course."

"I see." I turned to Mr. Broberg, "Mr. Thiel, may I have a few days to think about this?"

"Of course, young man, of course." We rose to leave, a few of the partners rose to shake my hand and apologize personally about eight months late.

Settlement

I wrestled with my feelings about my old firm. Of course, they were entitled, educated people who represented money interests. An easy answer. They cared little for the practice of law or integrity. They served on charitable boards to make contacts for business, they contributed to political campaigns en masse to gain political influence and business, they joined clubs to hobnob with people to get business. They befriended judges to get favorable rulings. They were a business entity without a collective soul or conscience. Easy. But what was I? I spent months in prison because two of the firm without a second thought set me up for a crime I did not commit, so they could steal $3.1 million. But I unraveled the plot. Ms. Hollister gave me a key. Reggie and Tariq/Leon helped me. Somehow events were guided. Most of all, I learned. I did not want to be a member of that type of law firm. They were not my people. They cast me into a pit and left me for dead, but I arose. I arose by helping others without being asked, just because it was in my nature. What was my nature – to seek power, no, that lust for power, to seek prestige – who needed that? Who was I impressing? It was as if I had been freed by the unintentional acts of the law firm. No. I did not need revenge. It was enough to see the scared faces of the partners, not a true grimace of apology or remorse, only personal fear.

I got that. No, I didn't need revenge on these sad men. But the money would be nice. I mean, I'm not stupid. I called Broberg.

"Jake, what can I do?"

"Anything over $50 million I'll take."

"We can do better than that."

206

"I'm sure, but I want it to be over, I want it now. I want my life back. Do what you do." I went to the gym and left my cell phone on. As always, the gym was my meditation zone. I worked out with the blue collar guys, kibitzed and pumped iron. The cell rang.

"Jake, I got $65 million, no lawsuit. We release everyone at the bank and the law firm, including Gardner and Chatsworth. Only we weren't settling with Mittendorf. But they won't have any money left after they are found guilty. They have to make restitution, pay their lawyers."

"That's fine, Jake. Good job. Nice work. Somehow the money felt good, but it hadn't sunk it. I went over to the lat machine and pumped out a dozen. If anything I felt free.

THE FOUNDATION

My criminal lawyer, Joe Hirshberg, called as soon as he heard about the settlement. He was getting $100,000 as a referral fee for a single phone call to Bonafine and Broberg. He had been told the referral fee was to kick back over $20 mil. What did I want to do with that? No sweat on that decision. I wanted a charitable foundation set up for prison reform – access to computers, trade schools, gym equipment, and social agencies to find jobs. Reggie and Tariq would serve on the board, along with me and with an ex-warden and a senior social worker. I wanted him to consult a trust specialist and get it drawn up.

Now, I was worth about $48 million. Since none of it was repayment of lost wages, it was tax free – pure pain and suffering, loss of reputation, punitive damages.

What was I going to do next? I walked over to the leg press machine and did a dozen pumps. Then I got dressed and went next door for a cheese steak, sauce and onions and a diet root beer. Maybe I'd go to Europe for a while, rethink my life.

AFTERMATH

I still felt a bit numb. I had plenty of money, more than I would ever need. Somehow, it robbed me of the incentive to scratch and claw my way up the financial ladder. I had also seen my enemies brought low. This also gave me little satisfaction. Revenge is a fine idea when you do not yet have it, but when your enemies suffer downfall and humiliation, it is surprisingly little comfort. All their sentences and financial suffering affected me only to a slight degree. Gardner was a _____ stupid shnook who would spend a large amount of time in jail and leave his wife destitute with young children to support. Chatsworth had taken a huge dumb risk when he had no reason to gamble on his already assured financial and professional success; it was perhaps inevitable that his high riding lifestyle would bring him down. His wife while lacking grace or manners would nonetheless survive to marry and live again. Mittendorf had been able to navigate in the world using popularity and his wife's social and financial connections. Other than simply enjoy the gifts he had gotten, he chose to gamble and deserved to lose. Haynesworth was a soldier for the moneyed interests, he fought the way he knew how to protect the law firm by trying to button up the scandal. He went down like a solider, but suffered little loss. Hawley was a jerk vomited up by the system, and now exposed as a pitiful, stupid drunk.

No, on the whole, I had little emotion invested in their downfall. What I did recognize was the support I received from my prison friends. They were grateful for the help I provided, and the prison community repaid me. It was amazing how this group of discarded souls had used their street smarts which they had acquired instead of book learning for my benefit. They deserved by return gratitude. I looked into each of their cases to see what could be done, but some combination of poor upbringing, deficient schools, and poor personal choices had doomed them early in life. I did the best I could for them – parole board representation, social workers, job training – but their lives were not easily salvaged. I expanded my efforts to the rest of the state prisons. That was the least I could do.

In the meantime, I found myself rejecting my previously planned interests. The country club, Bonnie, were things of the past. I saw how quickly they could reject me if I had a broken wing. I found that I derived far greater satisfaction in supporting the underserved in the legal part of the equation. Those who needed legal and financial advice but got caught up in a system where they – the most needy – got the least help. It was there that I met Francine, a very energetic manager of a non-profit that did exactly that. But that is a story for another day.